P9-CMA-350

STORIES IN HISTORY

THE CIVIL WAR

1860–1865

nextext

Printed in China
ISBN-13: 978-0-618-14214-9
ISBN-10: 0-618-14214-2

7 8 9 10 NPC 09 08 07 06

Table of Contents

by Barbara Littman

*Robert E. Lee loves the army and army life. He
also loves his native state of Virginia. When the
war begins, agents for President Lincoln offer
Lee command of the Union armies. Lee faces
a difficult decision.*

PART II: BATTLE FRONT

PART III: BEHIND THE LINES

About this Book

The stories are historical fiction. They are based on historical fact, but some of the characters and events may be fictional. In the Sources section you'll learn which is which and where the information came from.

The illustrations are all historical. If they are from a time different from the story, the caption tells you. Original documents help you understand the time period. Maps let you know where things were.

Items explained in People and Terms to Know are repeated in the Glossary. Look there if you come across a name or term you don't know.

Historians do not always agree on the exact dates of events in the past, and in some cases records of exact dates were not kept. The letter c before a date means "about" (from the Latin word circa).

If you would like to read more about these exciting times, you will find recommendations in Reading on Your Own.

Background

The Battle Hymn of the Republic
(first stanza)

*Mine eyes have seen the glory of the coming of
    the Lord;
He is trampling out the vintage where the
    grapes of wrath are stored;
He hath loosed the fateful lightning of
    His terrible swift sword;
His truth is marching on.*

—Julia Ward Howe

God Save the South
(fourth stanza)

*Rebels before, our fathers of yore.
Rebel's the righteous name Washington bore.
Why, then, be ours the same,
The name that he snatched from shame,
Making it first in fame, foremost in war.
Making it first in fame, foremost in war.*

—Earnest Halpin

Why the Nation Went to War

America's Civil War (1861–1865) grew out of differences between its Northern and Southern states. The Southern states were mostly agricultural, growing cotton, tobacco, and other crops. In the South, slavery was legal, and millions of African slaves worked on the region's large plantations. Northern states were more industrial, with many well-developed cities. In the North, slavery was against the law. The Northern economy didn't need slaves. Foreign immigrants provided its labor supply.

Differences Over Slavery

Before the Civil War, sharp differences over the issue of slavery began to divide North and South. Most Northerners felt that slavery was wrong. They wanted it abolished [ended] throughout the country. This view angered most Southerners. Southerners insisted that slavery should remain legal. They felt that states, rather than the national government, should decide whether slavery would be allowed.

◀ Pickett's Charge at the Battle of Gettysburg.

By making cotton production profitable, the cotton gin helped preserve slavery in the South.

Attempts to Compromise Fail

In the 1800s, America expanded westward and new states joined the Union. The conflict over slavery became more heated. The North wanted more free states. The South wanted more slave states. In the U.S. Congress, North and South battled over this issue. Attempts to reach an agreement—the Missouri Compromise (1820) and the Compromise of 1850—failed to work in the long run. In 1854, the Kansas-Nebraska Act allowed states to settle the issue for themselves. But this didn't work either. In Kansas, two governments—slave and non-slave— fought for control. Blood was shed, and soon the state was being called "Bleeding Kansas."

The Nation Divides

Tension between North and South increased and the nation moved toward war. The conflict over slavery reached a climax in 1860. Republican Abraham Lincoln was elected president. Because the Republicans favored abolition, South Carolina withdrew from the Union. Within a few months, ten other Southern states also had left the Union. They formed the Confederate States of America and elected Jefferson Davis president. The nation was divided. War was about to begin.

Readiness for War: North vs. South

When the Civil War began, the North had many advantages over the South.

South	North
9 million people	22 million people
1 million who could fight	4 million who could fight
100,000 workers in industry	1,000,000 workers in industry
Almost no navy	25 times larger navy
Little iron production	15 times greater iron production
Few railroads	Better railroads
Little firearms production	32 times greater firearms production

The South started in a weak position. But it had good military leaders and a strong fighting spirit. It also hoped to get money and arms from England and France.

Important Battles and Events

In the Civil War's first phase (1861–1863), Confederate forces under Robert E. Lee were on the attack. The Confederate armies often defeated the disorganized and weakly led Union army. In the second phase (1863–1865), a forceful new Union leader, General Ulysses S. Grant, led Union forces to the final victory.

These are the major events of the war:

April 12, 1861 **Start of the War.**
Confederates fire on and capture Union-held Fort Sumter, South Carolina.

July 1861 **First Battle of Bull Run.**
Confederate armies stop an over-confident Union army from taking Richmond, Virginia, the Confederate capital.

September 17, 1862 **Antietam.**
Union General George McClellan stops Lee's invasion of Maryland. This is the bloodiest single day of the war.

January 1, 1863 **Emancipation Proclamation.**
Lincoln's measure allows Union troops to free slaves and lets blacks serve in the Union army.

May 1863 **Chancellorsville.**
The South wins the battle, but "Stonewall"
Jackson, one of its best generals, is killed.

July 1863 **Gettysburg and Vicksburg.**
Lee invades Pennsylvania but loses at Gettysburg.
General Grant takes Vicksburg, giving Union forces
control of the Mississippi. This is the turning point
of the war.

May 1864 **Grant's Final Strategy.**
Grant begins a drive to wear down Lee's forces
and take Richmond.

May 1864–March 1865 **Union March to the Sea.**
Union General William Tecumseh Sherman
marches through Georgia and the Carolinas,
burning cities, destroying railroads and crops,
and looting homes.

April 9, 1865 **Confederate Surrender.**
Robert E. Lee surrenders at the village of Appomattox
Court House. On April 14, Lincoln is shot while
watching a play and dies the next morning.

December 1865 **End of Slavery.**
Twenty-seven states ratify the Thirteenth
Amendment, abolishing slavery in the United States.

Civil War Strategy, 1861–1865

How the War Was Fought

When the war began, the North's goals were to close Southern ports, to cut the Confederacy in half by controlling the Mississippi River, and to capture its capital, Richmond. The Confederate plan was to invade the North and defeat the Union armies. Both sides had to change their plans as the war went on.

During the Civil War, 3 million men fought nearly 150 major battles, on land and at sea. Railroads brought supplies to Northern forces. Steamboats helped supply the South.

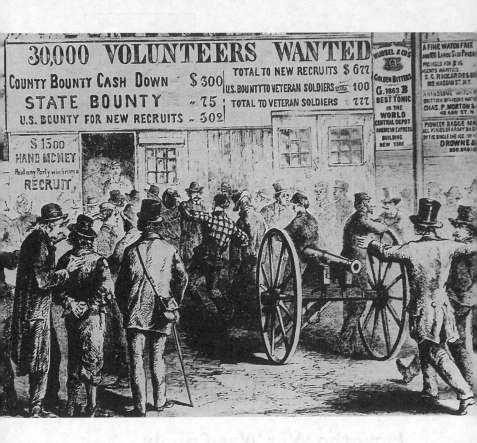

▲
A billboard in New York City calls for volunteers for the Union Army.

Battle Lines

In land battles, long lines of defenders usually faced the long lines of attackers across an open field. Sometimes the defenders were in rifle pits—trenches lined at the top by logs that had slits to fire through.

The attacking side, led by officers, moved forward to the beat of drums. The Confederates often ran toward the enemy with a terrifying "rebel yell."

As defenders fired on them, attacking soldiers had to stop to fire and reload their rifles. Most Civil War soldiers used five-foot-long rifles that loaded at the barrel. These rifles could fire three rounds per minute to about 400 yards. Later on, better guns became available. Soldiers also used hand grenades and mines. They were supported by troops on horseback and by gun crews firing cannons.

War at Sea

The Union and Confederate navies were very active during the war. For the first time, steam-powered boats replaced sailing ships. Most Civil War ships were wooden. But both navies used "ironclads"— ships that were protected by sheets of iron. Some had revolving guns. Confederate inventors developed the first submarine. It sank a Union ship in Charleston Harbor.

The North had more ships—670 by war's end. Early in the war it blockaded, or closed, ports along the entire 3,500-mile Confederate coastline. This blockade became more effective as the war went on.

Civil War Photography

During the early 1800s, photography was just coming into use. A young New Yorker named Mathew Brady (1823–1896) started taking photos of famous people, including many presidents. In 1844, Brady opened his first photo gallery in New York City. Almost overnight, he became

▲
Alexander Gardner, who worked with Mathew Brady, photographed these dead Confederates after the battle of Antietam in September 1862.

wealthy and famous, though he was only 21 years old.

When the Civil War started, Brady decided to create a photographic record of the conflict. This had never been done before. Later, Brady said, "A spirit in my feet said 'Go' and I went." Brady hired twenty photographers and sent them throughout the war zone. Brady himself photographed the battles of Bull Run, Antietam, and Gettysburg. He also photographed Lincoln in the field and Robert E. Lee just after he surrendered.

People were shocked by Brady's scenes of battles and death. After a Brady exhibit called "The Dead of Antietam," a reporter wrote, "Mr. Brady has done something to bring to us the terrible reality and earnestness of the war. If he has not brought bodies and laid them in our door-yards and along our streets, he has done something very like it."

Brady spent $100,000 of his own money on the Civil War project. It ruined him financially. He had hoped that the government would pay him when the war ended. Brady finally got a payment of $25,000, but he died alone in a charity ward.

The War's End and Aftermath

Bankrupt in men, in money, & in provisions,
the wail of the bereaved & the cry of hunger
rising all over the land, Our cities burned with
fire and our pleasant things laid waste, the best
& bravest of our sons in captivity, and the
entire resources of our country exhausted—
what else could we do but give up.

—Sarah Hine, a woman from Georgia

More than 620,000 Americans died in the Civil War. Another 600,000 were wounded. Historians estimate that the Union and Confederate governments spent about $20 billion in fighting each other.

The outcomes were simple. After the North won the war, the Confederate states became part of the Union again. The Thirteenth Amendment ended slavery in America. But the South was bitter. Four years of war had destroyed many of its cities and much of its farmland, its livestock, and its forests. The South had been forced to give up the slaves that had made it a wealthy land. It took generations to heal the wounded hearts of those who lost.

▲
When the war ended in 1865, much of the South (like Charleston, South Carolina, shown here) was in ruins.

Time Line

1818—Slave and non-slave states are balanced at 10 each.

1820—The Missouri Compromise is adopted.

1845—Texas is admitted to the Union as a slave state.

1849—California forbids slavery.

1850—The Compromise of 1850, including the Fugitive Slave Act, is enacted.

1854—The Kansas–Nebraska Act permits slavery north of $36°30'$.

1855—Slavery supporters and abolitionists organize rival governments in Kansas.

1857—The *Dred Scott* decision makes the Missouri Compromise unconstitutional.

1860—Abraham Lincoln wins the presidential election; South Carolina secedes.

1861–1865—The Civil War is fought.

1865—The Thirteenth Amendment to the U.S. Constitution outlaws slavery.

Leaders

Robert E. Lee's Decision

BY BARBARA LITTMAN

He dipped his pen in the ink, ready to sign his name. He couldn't believe it had come to this. Glancing out the window over the peaceful Virginia landscape, **Robert E. Lee** could see as far as Washington, D.C.

There he could see many of the buildings that were symbols of the country he loved: the unfinished Washington Monument, the spires of the great Smithsonian Museum, and even the Capitol dome, still under construction.

People and Terms to Know

Robert E. Lee—(1807–1870) commander of the Southern armies during the Civil War and a Confederate hero.

Mathew Brady photographed General Lee in April 1865, following the surrender of the Confederacy.

Lee sighed. He had many reasons to be loyal
to the U.S. government. Two Lees had signed the
Declaration of Independence. His
father had been a famous leader
during the Revolutionary War. Lee
himself had graduated second in his
class at the U.S. Military Academy
at West Point. Now he was a U.S.
army colonel who had served in the
Mexican War. But he felt he had to give all that up.

*Two Lees had
signed the
Declaration of
Independence.*

He reread his letter to Simon Cameron, the
Secretary of War.

"S ir:

"I have the honor to tender [offer] the resignation of my commission as Colonel of the 1st Regt.
of Cavalry.

"Very resp'y [respectfully] Your Obedient Servant."

Now he must sign his name. He dipped his pen
one more time and signed the letter. On April 20,
1861, Lee resigned from the U.S. army.

People and Terms to Know

Mexican War—(1846–1848) war between Mexico and the United
States. The war began when Mexico refused to accept the 1845 United
States annexation of Texas. After winning the war, the United States
acquired Mexican territory from the Rio Grande River to the Pacific
coast.

For the last several weeks, Lee had held on to the hope that he would not need to take this step. On April 4, his state, Virginia, in a state convention had voted not to **secede** from the **Union**. It would not join South Carolina and the six other states that had seceded in February. They had formed the **Confederate States of America**.

Within days, the picture changed. Back in December 1860, when South Carolina seceded, it had demanded that all federal property within its borders be handed over. President Buchanan had refused to order the federal troops to leave the fort at Charleston Harbor. So last week, on April 14, Confederate forces took over **Fort Sumter**. The fort had been unprepared for an attack. It was in bad repair and was manned by only 128 Union officers and men. It had been an easy victory for the Confederates.

People and Terms to Know

secede (sih•SEED)—withdraw from the Union. Some Southern states believed they had the right to separate from the United States and form their own national government.

Union—states that remained in the United States during the Civil War.

Confederate States of America—government formed by the eleven states that withdrew, or seceded, from the Union during the Civil War.

Fort Sumter—fort at the mouth of the harbor of Charleston, South Carolina. The first shots of the Civil War were fired here on April 12, 1861.

When the new president, **Abraham Lincoln**, heard the news, he ordered Virginia to send troops to take back the fort. Many Virginians did not want to obey.

Even though the Virginia state convention had voted to remain in the Union, many Virginians favored secession. With so much disagreement, the state convention met once more on April 17. "Should the state stay in the Union or secede?" That was the question to be voted on.

While the convention was debating, Lee had been called to Washington. He went to meet with two very important people. One was Francis P. Blair, a friend of President Lincoln. Blair was an important man in Washington who had great influence in the government. The other person who had called him was General **Winfield Scott**. Lee had served under General Scott in the Mexican War. Scott described Lee as the "the best soldier in Christendom," and he wanted him on the Union side.

People and Terms to Know

Abraham Lincoln—(1809–1865) 16th president of the United States (1861–1865). Lincoln wanted to hold the Union together, but South Carolina seceded from the Union when Lincoln's election was announced.

Winfield Scott—(1786–1866) U.S. army officer who was a hero of the War of 1812 and the Mexican War. When the Civil War broke out, 75-year-old Scott briefly commanded the Union army but soon retired.

Lee rode down Arlington Hill, over Long Bridge, and past the half-finished Washington Monument. He stopped at 1652 Pennsylvania Avenue, got off his horse, and rang the bell of Blair's stately Washington home.

When Lee and Blair were settled in the library, Blair offered him the post of commander of the Union army. Lee knew the offer had come from the president himself. He knew it was a great honor, and he loved his country.

He could never lead the Union army onto the soil of his native state!

Still, Lee was troubled. He knew that if Virginia seceded, he must follow. He could never lead the Union army onto the soil of his native state! If he did, he would be fighting friends, neighbors, and family. He had to refuse the offer.

After seeing Blair, Lee visited his old commander, General Scott. Scott was also from Virginia but he had decided to stay with the Union. For many months, Scott had been trying to get Lee to commit himself to the Union. But now Lee told him that he had refused Blair's offer. He would go with Virginia if it seceded. With a sigh, Scott recommended that he resign from the U.S. army.

With a heavy heart, Lee left the capital to return home to Virginia. On the way, he heard rumors that the convention had voted for secession. The next day, in the Alexandria *Gazette* headline he read that it was true. Virginia had seceded.

Now he would fight for the state of Virginia against the country he loved.

That is how Lee found himself sitting at his writing desk with a letter of resignation in front of him. From the moment he signed the letter, he was no longer a colonel in the U.S. army. Worse, now he would fight *for* the state of Virginia *against* the country he loved.

It was a sad irony. Even though Lee had a great war record, he disliked war. He had always hoped that the North and South could resolve their differences without shedding blood. He was also against slavery. He had only owned a few slaves in his lifetime—and those only briefly. They were a gift from his father-in-law. Lee had freed the slaves as soon as he got them. Yet now he would fight on the side of the Southern slave states.

▲
Confederate horsemen rest during Lee's first invasion of the North in September 1862.

Lee pushed back his chair and stood up. He must go downstairs and tell his wife, Mary, what he had done. With the letter in hand, he passed the painting of Martha Washington, the camp furniture from the Revolutionary War, and the other reminders of his love for his country that decorated his house. This had been the hardest decision he had made in his life. But he knew that Mary would understand.

By Monday, Lee was in Richmond, the capital of Virginia. There he was appointed commander of all the state's forces. As commander, with the rank of major general, Lee would be fighting alongside many of the brave men he had fought with in the Mexican War. The group included **Thomas J. "Stonewall" Jackson**, John Magruder, Richard Ewell, and **P.G.T. Beauregard**.

Lee also would be fighting against other brave men who had fought alongside him in the Mexican War. These men were **George B. McClellan**, Joseph Hooker, John Pope, **Ambrose E. Burnside**, and **Ulysses S. Grant**. (Lee would eventually surrender to Grant when the Confederacy could no longer hold out against Union forces.)

People and Terms to Know

Thomas J. "Stonewall" Jackson—(1824–1863) U.S. general, widely considered one of the best Confederate commanders. He received the nickname "Stonewall" at the First Battle of Bull Run (1861). There, his troops stood against the Union forces "like a stone wall."

P.G.T. Beauregard (BOH•rih•GAHRD)—(1818–1893) Confederate general who commanded the attack on Ft. Sumter that opened the Civil War. Though successful in many other battles, he was driven out of Charleston by General Sherman.

George B. McClellan—(1826–1885) U.S. general and commander of the Union army during the first year of the Civil War. Though McClellan did an exceptional job of organizing and training the army, Lincoln dismissed him for being too cautious.

Ambrose E. Burnside—(1824–1881) former firearms manufacturer who became a Union general during the Civil War. Burnside commanded troops at Bull Run and Antietam. In November 1862, Lincoln named Burnside commanding general, but he resigned after failing to win an important battle.

Ulysses S. Grant—(1822–1885) commander of the Union army. 18th president of the U.S. (1869–1877). Grant led Union forces to victory, but his presidency was marked by many scandals.

* * *

The Civil War lasted for four years, from 1861 to 1865. Even though the Confederacy lost, Robert E. Lee is considered a brilliant general. He was respected by both sides for his honor, intelligence, and decency.

Lee also won praise for the way he ended the war. After surrendering to Grant, he encouraged his fellow Southerners to rejoin the Union. He urged them to work to rebuild the country after the destructive war. His attitude influenced many Southerners to put aside their differences with the North. Lee himself took a low-paying job as president of Washington College so that he could help educate the next generation of patriotic Southerners.

QUESTIONS TO CONSIDER

1. How was Robert E. Lee's problem similar to that facing the Virginia state convention?

2. Why did Lee choose to fight for Virginia, even though he was against slavery?

3. How did Lee help the divided country to heal after he surrendered to Grant?

4. What do you think might have happened if Southerners and Northerners had not worked together after the war to rebuild the Union?

Robert E. Lee

Civil War historian Douglas Southall Freeman described Robert E. Lee at the time of Lee's decision to reject command of the Union army:

"He was then fifty-four years of age and stood five feet eleven inches in height, weighing slightly less than 170 pounds. In physique, he was sound. . . . he was possessed of great powers of endurance. When he was past forty, he had competed with his sons in high jumps at Arlington. He had skated and danced and had been an excellent swimmer. . . . In appearance, one [person] who saw him that April day, considered Lee 'the noblest looking man I had ever seen.' . . . His finest appearance was when mounted [on horseback], for he was an admirable rider. . . ."

—Douglas Southall Freeman, *Lee*

Unconditional Surrender Grant

BY STEPHEN FEINSTEIN

The last thing Jonathan remembered was the sound of the cannon shell that came screaming in just above the soldiers' heads. There was a loud explosion, and everything went black.

When Jonathan came to, he was lying on his back on a cot. He noticed a numbness all down his right leg. He had no idea how long he had lain there. When his eyes got used to the dim light in the first-aid tent, he saw that he was not alone. Other men lay on cots, some groaning in pain, some deathly silent. Jonathan reached down to feel his right leg, but he couldn't find it. Jonathan gasped with a horrible realization. His right leg was gone! Once again, Jonathan sank into a bottomless pool of blackness.

This photograph of General Grant was taken in 1862.

Jonathan awoke during the night. It was too dark to see much, although a candle flickered somewhere inside the tent. Jonathan was terribly thirsty, but he was too weak to cry out for water. He felt cold, even though a blanket covered him. It was quiet except for the moaning on the other side of the tent. Jonathan lay there alone with his thoughts. This was not what was supposed to happen to him. He had set out for the greatest adventure of his life. He had never really believed that something terrible could happen. Now he realized that he was lucky to be alive. Although he couldn't move, his mind was racing. He reviewed the events that had brought him to his present situation.

In the fall of 1861, 18-year-old Jonathan Portman answered the call to save the Union. He volunteered for duty in the Union army. Along with thousands of other volunteers, Jonathan had gone through long, dull months of military training. Once the volunteers had learned how to use their <u>muskets</u> and <u>bayonets</u>, they were ready for real

People and Terms to Know

muskets—long guns. Used from the 1500s to the 1800s. The musket's lead ball was fired by lighting a powder charge. Muskets were more than 5 feet long, weighed up to 40 pounds, and were not accurate beyond 100 yards.

bayonets (BAY•uh•netz)—stabbing weapons attached to long guns. The bayonet was a long, tapering, steel blade.

combat. They wondered when their great adventure was going to begin.

It finally began in early February 1862. Brigadier General Ulysses S. Grant was stationed at Cairo, Illinois. He was planning to stop the Confederates from moving northward. The forty-year-old general who would one day become commander of all the Union armies was eager to prove himself.

Grant's plan called for a joint army and navy operation.

Grant had earlier resigned from the army after a disappointing military career. He then had tried his hand at farming without much success. After working in his father's leather goods business for a year, Grant joined the army again. The Union needed him. He was immediately appointed brigadier general.

General Grant assembled his forces at Paducah, Kentucky. His first goal was to attack Fort Henry. The Confederates had built this fort on the Tennessee River, south of Paducah. Grant commanded twenty-three **regiments** with about 17,000 men. This included Jonathan's volunteer division, led by

People and Terms to Know

regiments—military units or bodies of troops.

General Charles F. Smith. Grant's plan called for a joint army and navy operation, with a fleet of gun boats, including four **ironclads**. Flag Officer Andrew H. Foote commanded the ships. Grant's troops were carried by steamers up the river.

As Jonathan sailed up the river with his regiment, he admired the ironclads. He had never seen such strange-looking boats. "Those are Pook Turtles," said a sailor. "They were designed by Samuel Pook, the naval engineer." Jonathan agreed that they looked like turtles, with those guns poking out of the front and sides. Jonathan laughed, imagining a turtle involved in a battle.

On February 6th, the troops went ashore three miles north of Fort Henry. They would march the rest of the way to the fort. Jonathan remembered how excited the men had been. But their good mood didn't last long. The soldiers had to slog through deep mud, which slowed them down.

People and Terms to Know

ironclads—naval boats of the mid-1800s. Ironclads were protected with iron plates on the sides. Famous Civil War ironclads were the *Monitor* and the *Merrimack*.

While they slogged, the gunboats quickly reached Fort Henry and began the attack. One of the ironclads, the *Essex*, was put out of action early by deadly fire from the fort. Many aboard were killed.

▲
Jonathan Portman's winter uniform would have been like the one worn by this Union sergeant.

This was the only Union loss. The Union **cannon** fire was intense and accurate. The Confederates could not take it for long. Besides, the river waters were rising and threatening to flood the fort. Before Jonathan's division arrived, the Confederates raised a white flag of surrender above the fort. That night, there was

This time, victory would not come so easily.

much celebrating among the army troops, even though they had "missed the fun," and the day's victory went to the navy.

Grant's next goal was to attack Fort Donelson on the Cumberland River, twelve miles from Fort Henry. Grant planned again to use the winning combination of naval gunboats and army regiments to capture the fort. But this time, victory would not come so easily. Fort Donelson was located on a 120-foot high bluff overlooking a bend in the river. About 20,000 enemy troops were stationed there.

On February 12th, Grant rode out from Fort Henry at the head of his troops. The day was unusually warm. Jonathan wore his heavy over-

---

People and Terms to Know

cannon—large gun, especially one that is too large to be carried by hand, that is fixed to the ground or mounted on wheels. During the Civil War, cannons that shot cannonballs or exploding shells were used by both sides.

coat. He was sweating as he trudged along under the fifty-pound knapsack. Inside the pack were his woolen blanket and other supplies. He also carried his musket, bayonet, canteen, and cartridge box containing forty bullets. Men were grumbling from the heat. Suddenly, the tall soldier marching next to Jonathan stopped. He took off his overcoat and slammed it to the ground, along with his blanket. "Aren't you going to need your coat later?" asked Jonathan.

"I doubt it. Seems to me that spring is here. Anyhow, I'm sick and tired of carrying all these things around," said the soldier. Other soldiers saw what the tall soldier had done and quickly followed his lead. After trudging through the woods for another mile, Jonathan, too, threw away his overcoat and blanket. That was a mistake! That night, a cold front passed through. The temperature dropped sharply, and it became bitterly cold. Jonathan nearly froze to death. He had to keep moving about all night long on the frozen ground. He got no sleep.

On February 14th, Foote's ironclads began firing on Fort Donelson. They couldn't do much damage, however, because of the fort's superior firepower. Grant realized that the plan he had used at Fort Henry was not going to work here.

The morning of February 16th was bitter cold. Blustery winds blew icy sleet into the soldiers' faces. Jonathan shivered as he watched General Grant ride up on his horse. Grant gave an order to General Smith, Jonathan's commander. "You must take Fort Donelson!" said Grant to the white-haired general.

"I will do it," said Smith.

General Smith ordered Jonathan's regiment to charge the Confederate positions in front of the fort. The charge was interrupted by a huge **abatis** that blocked the volunteers' attack on the fort. Smith rode among the men, waving his sword and shouting at them. Jonathan would never forget his words: "Damn you, gentlemen. I see skulkers [cowards]!

> *"You volunteered to be killed for the love of your country, and now you can be."*

I'll have none here. . . . You volunteered to be killed for the love of your country, and now you can be. . . . I'm only a [professional] soldier and I don't want to be killed, but you came to be killed. . . ." Smith's strong words worked on the men. They swarmed over the abatis, shouting and firing their muskets at

---

People and Terms to Know

abatis (AB•UH•tihs)—barricade formed by stacking cut-down trees with sharpened branches to stop the advance of the enemy.

the defenders behind it. The fort rose up above them. Again Jonathan heard in his mind the awful sound of the cannon shell coming at him. That was the frightful moment just before everything went black. He would relive this moment many times in his nightmares.

Jonathan finally fell asleep just before dawn. When he awoke, sunlight was streaming into his tent. Bodies were being removed. Many soldiers, some no older than Jonathan, had given their lives to save the Union. A medical orderly who was helping to care for the wounded saw Jonathan watching him. He asked him, "How are you feeling?" The orderly then explained, "Sorry, we had to take your leg. It was terribly mangled. **Gangrene** would have set in."

"Say," said the orderly, "did you hear how your battle came out? People have given U.S. Grant a new name—'Unconditional Surrender Grant!'"

"So Grant is not the one who surrendered?" asked Jonathan.

People and Terms to Know

Gangrene (GANG•green)—death and decay of body tissue due to loss of blood supply.

▲

A Union surgeon performs an operation in a field hospital at Gettysburg, July 1863.

"Correct," said the orderly. "Everyone's celebrating. This is our first major victory in the war. We took almost 15,000 prisoners. I heard that's the largest number ever captured in one battle on this continent! Do you know what Grant said to the troops afterward? He said, 'Fort Donelson will hereafter be marked in capitals on the maps of our united country, and the men who fought the battle will live in the memory of a grateful people.'"

A mix of pride and regret swept through Jonathan. "How did the surrender come about?" he asked.

"Well, there were three Confederate generals at Fort Donelson. When it was clear that our boys had the upper hand, generals John Floyd and Gideon Pillow escaped. They left behind the third in command, General **Simon Bolivar Buckner**, to surrender to the Union army. Buckner sent a message to Grant, asking to discuss the terms of surrender. Grant sent back a note saying, 'No terms except unconditional and immediate surrender can be accepted.'

"After the surrender, Grant and Buckner were overheard talking and laughing together about old times. It seems that the two were old friends who had fought together in the war against Mexico."

Jonathan understood that friend against friend, even brother against brother, would become all too common in this war. But this was a situation that Jonathan would never have to face. For him, the war was over.

People and Terms to Know

Simon Bolivar (boh•LEE•vahr) **Buckner**—(1823–1914) Confederate general and, later, governor of Kentucky from 1887 to 1891.

QUESTIONS TO CONSIDER

1. Why did Jonathan volunteer for duty in the Union army?

2. What was General Grant's plan in attacking Fort Henry?

3. Why were Grant's winning tactics at Fort Henry unsuccessful at Fort Donelson?

4. How did General Smith rouse the volunteers under his command?

5. How did U.S. Grant earn his new name?

6. How is a civil war different from other kinds of wars?

The Story of the Battle of Shiloh
by Zachary Kent

U. S. Grant's toughness as a commander was shown at the bloody two-day battle of Shiloh. By nightfall of the first day, Union forces were nearly beaten. But Grant held on, and the next day the Confederates were forced to retreat. Zachary Kent presents an account of Shiloh.

Vicksburg:
The Battle That Won the Civil War
by Mary Ann Fraser

Vicksburg was the last major Confederate stronghold on the Mississippi River. Grant's capture of the city in July 1863 split the South in two, bringing Union victory closer. Mary Ann Fraser uses the writings of people who were present at Vicksburg to tell the story of this critical Civil War battle.

Unconditional Surrender:
U. S. Grant and the Civil War
by Albert Marrin

Albert Marrin's biography presents a full account of the life and career of U. S. Grant, who led the Union armies to victory in the Civil War and became the 18th president of the United States.

The Other President

BY WALTER HAZEN

Journal Entry

December 7, 1889

Jefferson Davis died yesterday in New Orleans. May he rest in peace. And may future historians be kinder to him than those who presently tear him down.

I first met Jeff Davis at Transylvania College in Lexington, Kentucky. The year was 1824. How young we both were: sixteen! He didn't stay in Lexington long. His older brother Joseph got him an appointment to the U.S. Military Academy at West Point, New York. From there, he went on to a career that began with a brief stay in the U.S. army

People and Terms to Know

Jefferson Davis—(1808–1889) president of the Confederate States of America (1861–1865).

Mathew Brady photographed Jefferson Davis before the war.

and ended with his becoming president of the Confederacy. As for myself, I became a lawyer. But I managed to stay in touch with Jeff through the years.

I remember Jeff's heartache when his first wife, Sarah, died. She was the daughter of **Zachary Taylor**, who had been his commanding officer at Fort Crawford, Wisconsin. She died of malaria only about three months after their wedding. Jeff almost died of the same illness, he told me in a letter after he'd recovered. After years of mourning, he married a second wife, Varina Howell. She was the daughter of a wealthy Southern planter. She and Jeff were married for more that forty years.

I followed Jeff's career after he left West Point. He fought in the **Black Hawk War** and later in the Mexican War. In between, he served as a U.S. congressman from Mississippi. Later, he was elected to the Senate and then appointed secretary of war in

---

People and Terms to Know

Zachary Taylor—(1784–1850) 12th president of the United States (1849–1850), serving only one year before dying of a stomach illness. Taylor had been an army hero, called "Old Rough and Ready" by his troops.

Black Hawk War—(1832) series of battles with the Sac and Fox Indians of Illinois. U.S. policy was to remove the Indians east of the Mississippi to lands to the west. When the Indian leader Black Hawk brought his people back, war broke out.

President Pierce's **cabinet**. He was again representing Mississippi in the Senate when the Civil War broke out.

Jeff was no raving **secessionist** like many Southerners. He was, to be sure, a strong supporter of states' rights. And he thought that slavery should be permitted in the western territories. But when Mississippi seceded and he gave up his seat in the Senate, he left with a feeling of great sadness. In his farewell speech, he urged North and South to make peace. His letters to me, though, expressed his fear that this would not be resolved peacefully.

In his farewell speech, he urged North and South to make peace.

Jeff came home to Brierfield, his large plantation twenty miles down the Mississippi River from Vicksburg. I visited him there on February 10, 1861. I remember the date because it was the day the telegram arrived from the Confederate convention in Montgomery, Alabama. It was a date that changed Jeff's life forever.

People and Terms to Know

cabinet—group of officials who head the major departments of government and advise the president.

secessionist (sih•SEHSH•uh•nihst)—person who favored leaving the Union.

Jeff, Varina, and I were in the rose garden talking about the conflict between North and South when the messenger appeared. He handed Jeff a telegram, which Jeff immediately opened and read. Varina and I watched his face for any signs of its contents. We could see he was not happy with what he had read.

The telegram told Jeff that he had been elected president of the Confederate States of America. Had I been Jeff, I would have been very happy! But not Jeff. He saw himself as more of a military leader than a politician. What he really wanted was to command the Southern armies that would soon fight the Union. Varina also told me that she believed he was best suited for a military role. But that was not to be. Jeff had to be content with accepting the top position in the Confederate government.

One week after the telegram arrived, on February 18, 1861, Davis was sworn in as the Confederate president. The first thing he did was try to work out a peace with Washington. But Lincoln wouldn't meet with Davis's representatives. Two months later, the first shots of the Civil War were fired at Fort Sumter.

As president, Davis faced many problems. The South was a farming area. It had no army, navy, or weapons. Its white population was tiny, only one-fourth that of the North. The South had poor railroads, few factories, and no shipyards. In addition, those in the new Confederate government battled among themselves and were hard to work with.

Davis worked hard to make the Confederate cause win.

Still, Jeff quickly tried to get control of the situation. Though Jeff no longer had time to write regularly, I read in the newspapers that he sent agents to try to get arms and support from France and England. In July, he began to work closely with Robert E. Lee. Lee helped the South organize its military forces. With Lee's support, Davis worked hard to make the Confederate cause win.

To many people, Davis seemed cold and impersonal. His family and friends saw a warmer person. For example, he set up a type of self-government on his plantation. Slaves formed their own juries and tried fellow slaves for various crimes. Although he strongly defended slavery, Jeff believed that slaves should be treated kindly. He educated some of them and hoped to prepare them for citizenship.

I always thought that Jeff's undoing as president was that he did not understand politics. Jeff thought that his way was the only way. He was very stubborn. One could say he was downright pig headed! He argued with his cabinet. He argued with his congress. He was always at odds with his generals. He even failed to get along with his vice-president, **Alexander Stephens**. And he never gained the affection of his people, as Abraham Lincoln did.

But let me come to Jeff's defense, if I may. From the start, Jeff faced a losing battle. The North was much better equipped to win the war. Just as important, his own congress refused to give him enough power to carry out the war. Still, Jeff did what he could. After the **Battle of Gettysburg**, General Lee blamed himself for the loss and wanted to resign. Jeff persuaded Lee to stay, protesting that "our country could not bear to lose you."

Well, I don't need to tell you who won the War between the States. You know that. When the fighting

People and Terms to Know

Alexander Stephens—(1812–1883) vice-president of the Confederate States of America. As a U.S. representative from Georgia, Stephens opposed secession, but he sided with the South when Georgia left the Union.

Battle of Gettysburg—major battle of the Civil War, fought July 1–3, 1863, in Pennsylvania. Union forces under General George G. Meade defeated Lee, forcing him to retreat. The Union side lost about 23,000 men, the Confederate side about 25,000. This Union victory was a turning point in the war.

ended, Jeff was the only Confederate official to be arrested and imprisoned. He was held at Fort Monroe, Georgia, for two years. The Union charged him with treason, but he was never brought to trial. Some said that the U.S. government was afraid that a court would say that states had a right to secede under the Constitution.

Jefferson Davis was 81 when he died yesterday. I wish I could attend his funeral, but my poor health prevents it. Thinking back on his life, I don't see Jeff as the "monster" many Northerners thought he was. He was a man who was loyal to the South, and he put all of his energy into trying to help the South.

I still have an *Atlantic Monthly* article about Jeff from September 1864. In it, a Northern writer said, "Our interview with him explained why, with no money and no commerce, with nearly every one of their important cities in our hands, and with an army greatly inferior in numbers and equipment to ours, the **Rebels** have held out so long. It is because of the sagacity [wisdom], energy, and indomitable will of Jefferson Davis."

People and Terms to Know

Rebels—those who fight against the legal government. In this case, Rebels means soldiers of the Confederate army who fought to set up a separate nation.

Jefferson Davis

John Peyton, an agent who represented North Carolina in England, visited the Confederate government in Richmond early in the war. He described President Davis:

"In person Mr. Davis is tall and slender—. . . 'a raw-boned man'—with a small, fine head, blue eyes, one of which is defective because of a wound he received at the battle of Buena Vista, . . . he has a high narrow forehead, ...

"Mr. Davis always impressed me as a man of abilities, but engaged in an enterprise, the foundation of an empire, far too difficult for any energies he possessed; as a man by no means stamped by nature with power and genius as his situation and the great crisis demanded. His whole manner of bearing was that of one almost stunned by what was passing before his astonished vision, and incapable of safely controlling and directing the vessel of state, amidst the winds and waves of the tempest."

QUESTIONS TO CONSIDER

1. How did Jefferson Davis feel about slavery? What was his view about extending it to the western territories?

2. What do you think were the reasons the delegates in Montgomery invited Davis to be their president? What qualifications did he have?

3. What problems did Davis face as president of the Confederacy? How did he handle these problems?

4. What is your opinion on the question of whether or not Jefferson Davis was a traitor?

Mr. Lincoln's Humor

BY JUDITH LLOYD YERO

Few people would expect the serious looking Abraham Lincoln shown in the statues at the Lincoln Memorial and at Mount Rushmore to have a great sense of humor. He led the country during one of the most difficult periods in history—the Civil War. Yet Lincoln was known for his jokes and humorous stories. His critics accused him of "lowering the dignity of the presidential office." But Lincoln used humor for very good reasons. The burden of the war weighed very heavily on the president. Humor helped him to keep up his spirits. He once explained to a friend, "I laugh because I must not weep—that's all, that's all."

This pro-Lincoln political cartoon makes fun of the shortness of his opponent
in the 1864 presidential election, General George McClellan.

Lincoln also felt that he was responsible for helping national **morale** during the war. He believed that his stories were "good to cheer up people in this hard world."

Lincoln had polished his storytelling skills when he was a young lawyer in Springfield, Illinois. After court, the lawyers would gather at the local tavern. Lincoln would tell a story that would send everyone into gales of laughter. Then someone would challenge another lawyer to tell a better one or go home. This would continue until one or two o'clock in the morning. It was an early version of a comedy club.

His stories were like Aesop's fables. Each contained a lesson.

Rather than arguing about an issue, Lincoln used stories to make his point. His stories were like Aesop's fables. Each contained a lesson. When Lincoln ran for the U.S. Senate, he ran against **Stephen A. Douglas**. Douglas could be confusing when he described his views. Lincoln poked fun at

---

People and Terms to Know

morale (muh•RAL)—mental outlook, spirit, or confidence. The morale of a group of people is important to its success. A leader helps to keep people's morale high.

Stephen A. Douglas—(1813–1861) famous speaker who served both as representative and senator from Illinois. Lincoln debated Douglas when he ran for Douglas's Senate seat.

him by saying, "Has it not got down to . . . soup that was made by boiling the shadow of a pigeon that had starved to death?"

Lincoln often poked fun at himself as well. He once described his absent-mindedness by telling a story of an Englishman "who was so absent-minded that when he went to bed he put his clothes carefully into the bed and threw himself over the back of the chair."

When he was president, Mr. Lincoln loved to make jokes at the expense of his generals. When he was told that Rebels had captured one of his generals, he commented that he didn't mind the loss of the general as much as he did the loss of the horse. "I can make a much better **brigadier** in five minutes, but the horses cost a hundred and twenty-five dollars apiece."

On another occasion, someone asked Lincoln how many men the Rebels had in the field. He answered very seriously, "Twelve hundred thousand,

People and Terms to Know

brigadier (BRIG•uh•DEER)—brigadier general, one who commands a brigade, a military group of between 1,800 and 2,000 infantry soldiers.

Lincoln's face, in his last photograph, shows the terrible strain of the war.

according to the best authority." The questioner was shocked. This was many times more soldiers than anyone thought. Lincoln explained, "Yes, sir, twelve hundred thousand—no doubt about it. You see, all of our generals, when they get whipped, say the enemy outnumbers them three to one, and I must believe them. We have four hundred thousand men in the field, and three times four makes twelve. Don't you see it?"

An important judge needed a **pass** into Southern territory to visit a relative in Virginia. It was hard to get a pass because so many people used such passes to carry information about the Union army to the South. The judge was refused by both a general and by **Edwin M. Stanton**, Lincoln's secretary of war. Stanton told the judge to ask the president himself. When the president heard that everyone else had refused the man, he said, "Well, then, I can do nothing, for you must know that I have very little influence with this administration!"

Later, someone asked Lincoln for a pass to go to Richmond, the capital of the Confederacy. Lincoln replied by joking about the Union army's failure to capture Richmond. "I would be very happy to oblige you if my passes were respected; but . . . I have, within the last two years, given passes to two hundred and fifty thousand men to go to Richmond, and not one has got there yet."

People and Terms to Know

pass—document giving written permission to leave Union territory and enter Confederate territory. Passes were required for travel during times of war.

Edwin M. Stanton—(1814–1869) U.S. secretary of war under two presidents, Lincoln and Andrew Johnson.

In 1864, when Lincoln was running for his second term, a friend remarked that nothing could defeat him unless General Grant captured Richmond, ran for president, and was nominated. "Well," said the president, "I feel very much like the man who said he didn't want to die particularly, but, if he had got to die, that was precisely the disease he would like to die of."

One of Mr. Lincoln's favorite stories sums up the way people saw the president. It was a story that was told about him rather than one he told himself. Two **Quaker** women were discussing who would win the Civil War.

"I think," said the first, "that Jefferson Davis will succeed."

"Why does thee think so?" asked the second.

"Because Jefferson is a praying man."

"And so is Abraham a praying man," the second responded.

"Yes," said the first, "but the Lord will think Abraham is joking."

People and Terms to Know

Quaker—name given to a member of the Society of Friends, a religious group.

QUESTIONS TO CONSIDER

1. What did Lincoln's story about the soup made from a pigeon's shadow mean? What was he really saying about Douglas?

2. What did Lincoln mean when he said that he could "make" a much better brigadier in five minutes?

3. What did Lincoln mean when he told the story about the man dying of a particular disease?

4. What is your opinion of a president using humor and jokes during very serious situations such as a war?

READING ON YOUR OWN

Lincoln: A Photobiography
by Russell Freedman

Russell Freedman combines photographs and text to tell the story of Abraham Lincoln.

The Abraham Lincoln Joke Book
by Beatrice Schenk De Regniers

Beatrice Schenk De Regniers collects examples of the humor that was a central part of Abraham Lincoln's character.

Acquainted with Darkness
by Ann Rinaldi

Ann Rinaldi's historical novel takes place in Washington D.C. in 1865, during the chaos that follows the assassination of Abraham Lincoln.

Battle Front

Civil War Soldiers

BY STEPHEN CURRIE

The sound of **reveille** cut through the early morning mist. Jeremiah Dawes opened his eyes, groaned, and climbed out of his bedroll. His mood was as gray as the November day.

Nearly a year had gone by since he had enlisted in the Union army. Nearly a year, Jeremiah thought, pulling on his worn-out shoes, and nothing had happened. There had been nothing worth writing home about. He had been in no real battles. His regiment sat, and sat, and sat some more. Day after day, it was the same.

Jeremiah shivered and picked a few lice out of his bright red hair. He was weary of everything—

People and Terms to Know

reveille (REV•uh•lee)—bugle call used to awaken soldiers.

The mud, the rain, the crowded camp full of home-sick soldiers, the Virginia chill that never quite managed to kill the bugs that bothered him, and most of all the boredom.

He wished that something would happen.

Anything, he decided, would be better than more sitting.

*   *   *

Fletcher Whitfield rubbed his eyes. It had been a long and dull day, but there was still one important task to be done before lights out. He leaned forward across the board that doubled as a writing desk, and for a moment there was no sound in the tent but the scratching of pen against paper.

November 18, 1862

Dear Mother,

Another day has dawned here in Virginia and still nothing changes. We drill, we march, we water the horses. The enemy is just across the stream, but we do not attack, and neither does he.

It is odd. When I joined our Confederate army, I expected a battle every day. I would take aim at our

<u>Yankee</u> enemies and shoot them down, one after the next. For years to come they would talk about me, the great Kentuckian Fletcher Whitfield, who so bravely defended the honor of our great Southern nation.

But in real life, soldiering is a good deal duller than that.

Greet the family for me—even your sister Marjorie, whose boy Jeremiah has cast his lot with the North. I hate his choice. Still, we share the same blood, and that cannot be denied.

Your Loving Son,

Fletcher

Fletcher folded the letter, as always, and addressed it to his mother. Tomorrow, he would mail it.

Tomorrow, he hoped, life would be more interesting.

* * *

People and Terms to Know

Yankee—word used during the Civil War to describe all Northerners and Union soldiers. In the Revolutionary War, the British called the American patriots *Yankees*. The Americans adopted the term. Today, *Yankees* means people from the New England states of Maine, New Hampshire, Vermont, Massachusetts, Rhode Island, and Connecticut.

"**F**atty bacon and worm-filled <u>hardtack</u> for supper again," Jeremiah's friend, Tom Andrews, said with a sigh. "And weak coffee, too, I'll be bound."

Jeremiah tried to remember just why he had joined. It was not for the coffee—for the excitement, perhaps. Being a soldier meant seeing new places and people. Of course, it also meant preserving the Union. The Southern states had wanted to leave and set up their own country. That would never do!

Whatever his reason for joining, going to war had seemed like quite an adventure at first. Unfortunately, the sense of adventure was long gone.

"Some nights I have a dream," said Jeremiah. "It's not about bacon and hardtack. Instead we get what Mother fixes for family feasts back home in <u>Kentucky</u>, like steaming roasts, rich stews and hot pies—" He licked his lips, remembering.

"Family feasts?" Tom asked. "Do all your people support the Union?"

"I have a couple of uncles who side with the South," Jeremiah admitted. "And a cousin who's

People and Terms to Know

hardtack—dry bread made of flour and water. Civil War soldiers on both sides of the conflict often ate hardtack.

Kentucky—border state between the North and the South. Kentucky stayed in the Union during the Civil War, but many people there felt loyal to the South.

up and joined the Rebel army." A picture popped into his head: Tall, thin, dark-haired Fletcher was chasing him through Grandfather's cornfields. Fletcher was grabbing him with a war whoop and wrestling him to the ground. It was all in fun, of course.

Not like now.

He swallowed hard, wishing himself home. He wished that things were back as they'd been before he and Fletcher had joined different sides and become sworn enemies.

*　*　*

A cold day, Fletcher told himself. It was good to be in the tent and not outside this bitter evening. Luckily, the ink had not frozen solid. He dipped the pen into the inkwell and wrote.

November 19, 1862

Dear Mother,

Tomorrow afternoon I run with the **skirmishers**. It will be my first time. Our commander says to shoot any Yankee who approaches the oak tree on

People and Terms to Know

skirmishers—small groups of soldiers who stage attacks on enemy scouts or patrollers.

our side of the stream. I wonder if he means to start a battle.

Keep me—keep all those who fight for the South—in your prayers.

Am mightily nervous, but then this is what being a soldier means. Keep me—keep all those who fight for the South—in your prayers.

Your Loving Son,
Fletcher

He folded and addressed the letter and prepared for sleep. Tomorrow would come soon enough.

* * *

Patrol duty was never interesting, thought Jeremiah. "Climb the hill, cross the stream, walk along the far bank, cross back," he murmured to himself as he began his route for the thirtieth time. As long as he stayed away from the oak tree near the riverbend, he'd be all right. Some scouts had reported a bunch of Confederate skirmishers there.

The sun faded over the horizon as Jeremiah waded in the stream. His mind drifted toward his cousin. Fletcher was a Rebel. How had he and Fletcher become so different? Fletcher had grown up on a farm with slaves, while Jeremiah was a town boy. Perhaps that had pushed them to choose North or South. Was it family? Their mothers were sisters from Kentucky, but Fletcher's father had come from Confederate South Carolina, while Jeremiah's was from Unionist Ohio. Did that explain it?

Was slavery a good reason to fight and to risk death?

Or perhaps slavery was the answer, he thought as he walked along. Like many Rebels, Fletcher's family owned slaves. They thought slavery was a good thing. Like many Unionists, Jeremiah's family disagreed. Was slavery a good reason to fight and to risk death? Was it important enough to pit cousin against cousin?

Jeremiah turned quickly. Something had stirred in the bushes beside him. With a start, he saw that he had wandered far off course—and close to the oak tree.

From behind a bush there stepped a man in a coat of gray, musket at the ready. A tall, thin man, Jeremiah noticed as he turned to flee. He was a dark-haired man, a man who looked oddly familiar, even at a distance and in the dying light.

There was an explosion.

And then there was silence.

* * *

A Confederate soldier who was later killed at Gettysburg.

Slowly Fletcher reached for the pen and ink. What he had to say today would be hard. And yet he knew he had no choice. With war, you had to take the good with the bad.

Sometimes it was hard to tell which was which.

November 19, 1862

Dear Mother,

Today I shot a Yankee. The act filled me with feelings I cannot quite understand. I should be delighted. The man was on our land, and shooting a Yankee can only help the Southern cause—

And yet I feel uneasy. Perhaps because I saw him well enough to know that his hair was red, much like cousin Jeremiah's. Surely the man cannot have been he, yet putting a human face on the Yankee has made me think.

When next you see your sister, please tell her that I bear her son no ill will. And that I hope the war ends soon enough for us all to be a family again.

Your Loving Son,
Fletcher

He folded the letter and addressed it. And then, slowly, he put out the light.

QUESTIONS TO CONSIDER

1. What did Fletcher and Jeremiah think that being a soldier would be like?

2. How was the reality of army life different from what they imagined it would be?

3. In what ways were the two soldiers' reasons for joining the army the same? In what ways were they different?

4. What is your opinion about Jeremiah's question, "Was slavery a good reason to fight?"

5. How do you think that the story would have ended if Fletcher had known he was aiming at Jeremiah? Why do you think so?

Letter from Willie Greene

Fletcher Whitfield and his letters are fictional. However, many Civil War soldiers' letters exist. Willie Greene, a sharpshooter, was 17 when he signed up to join the Union army. He wrote:

August 17, 1862

Dear Mother,

I now sit down to write you a few lines. . . . I will [tell] you . . . what I have seen of the battle field.

I can now step outside my tent and look up on to the mountain and see right where the enemy had a battery stationed. The ground for two miles around here is covered with graves of soldiers killed and the carcasses of dead horses and, I tell you, if you want a good wholesome stink just go about 1/2 mile above here and there you will get it, for horses are very thick there where the cavalry made a dash and a shell flew in amongst them. There is not much to be seen, only horses and graves, excepting old cartridge boxes, haversacks, canteens, etc.

. . . It is now after taps so I guess I will close. Good night.

The Boys' War: Confederate and Union Soldiers Talk About the Civil War
by Jim Murphy

Many of the soldiers who served in the Civil War were very young. Jim Murphy uses quotes from their diaries and letters to present an account of their experiences.

Behind the Blue and Gray: The Soldier's Life in the Civil War
by Delia Ray

Delia Ray describes the daily lives of those who fought for the Union and the Confederacy.

The Drummer Boy of Vicksburg
by G. Clifton Wisler

G. Clifton Wisler's historical novel is based on the experiences of a real-life Union drummer boy, Orion Howe, a 14-year-old who joined an Illinois regiment and received the Medal of Honor for heroism during the battle of Vicksburg.

Loreta Velazquez Becomes Lieutenant Harry Buford

BY WALTER HAZEN

March 30, 1880

Dear Inez,

I have just finished reading Loreta's book, *The Woman in Battle*. You must read it. If you do, write and tell me what you think.

Some people believe that Loreta made up much of her story. General **Jubal Early** is one of them. He says that Loreta could not have done all the things she claimed to have done and been to all the places she spoke of. I wonder.

People and Terms to Know

Jubal Early—(1816–1894) Confederate general. Like General Lee, he was against secession but was loyal to Virginia. He stayed a Rebel all his life and never promised loyalty to the United States after the war. Early claimed that Loreta Velazquez had made up much of her book.

This illustration from her own account of her career as a soldier shows
Loreta Velazquez disguised as Lieutenant Harry Buford.

More than 25 years have passed since we knew Loreta at the convent school in New Orleans. If you remember, she was from a wealthy Spanish family in Cuba, and she had been sent to New Orleans to go to school. I remember some of our conversations as though they happened yesterday. In history class, Loreta's heroine always was Joan of Arc, the young girl who led the French army against England. I remember Loreta saying that she wished she could be like Joan and fight glorious battles. She said that she wished she had been born a man. Remember how funny that seemed?

Loreta's heroine always was Joan of Arc, the young girl who led the French army against England.

Wasn't it in 1856 that we last saw her? I will never forget the day she ran away to marry that young army officer. How she met him I never knew, and I never knew his name. Did you? She does not even mention his name in her book.

When the war broke out in 1861, Loreta and her husband were at Fort Leavenworth, Kansas. This is certainly true, as well as the events that immediately followed. Loreta was upset and heartsick when her husband left to fight for the Confederacy. She made up her mind to follow him. To do so, she decided to disguise herself as a man.

Loreta describes in detail how she went about changing her identity. First she cut off her long dark hair. Remember how pretty it was? Then she glued on a mustache and a small beard. In no time at all, Loreta Velazquez became Lieutenant Harry T. Buford of the Confederate army.

But there's more. To better pass herself off as a man, Loreta decided she had to master doing "man" things. She practiced talking in a deep voice. She learned to walk in a manly way. She started chewing tobacco. She learned how to spit! How awful it must be to have a mouthful of tobacco! But I guess Loreta thought such a habit would make her disguise more believable.

Loreta goes on to say that the last thing she had to do was get fitted for an officer's uniform. She did this in Memphis, Tennessee. After that, she supposedly crossed over into Arkansas and organized a company of men. Then she had them transported to Pensacola, Florida, where her husband was at the time. Do you think she herself paid to move those fellows that distance?

Anyhow, Loreta soon reached Pensacola. You can imagine how shocked her husband was to learn that Lieutenant Buford was really his wife! But he went along with her game and told no one. He even named her as one of his aides and let her stay. Then a terrible thing happened. Shortly after she arrived, her husband was killed in a firearms demonstration. What a dreadful shock his death must have been for her.

Can you believe she was once hired by the Union to search for herself?

Instead of going home after this tragedy, Loreta decided to continue being Lieutenant Buford. Somehow she ended up at the **First Battle of Bull Run**. Some people doubt this part of her story. But after the war many Confederate soldiers said that they remembered a Lieutenant Buford fighting at Bull Run. Why would these men say that if she had not in fact been there?

In time, Loreta's true identify was discovered. After that, she became a spy. There is certainly enough evidence to support this claim. She also seems to have been a double agent for a time, working for both sides. Can you believe she was once hired by the Union to search for herself? Loreta claims that she was.

People and Terms to Know

First Battle of Bull Run—Civil War battle fought on July 21, 1861, at Bull Run Creek in Virginia, twenty-five miles southwest of Washington, D.C. Here Confederate General P.G.T. Beauregard defeated Union soldiers under General Irvin McDowell, but did not go after them as they retreated to Washington.

I often wonder what happened to Loreta. I know she traveled around after the war, talking about her life and her book. After that, she just dropped out of sight. Looking back on her story, I think we have to accept some of it as true and some of it as false. I've read that more than 400 women disguised themselves as soldiers and fought in the war. So the fact that Loreta became Harry Buford and marched off to the battlefield is not that unusual.

Remember, Inez, if you read Loreta's book, let me know your thoughts. And give my regards to your family.

Your devoted friend,
Maria

QUESTIONS TO CONSIDER

1. Why do you think General Early claimed that Loreta's story was hard to believe?

2. Why did Loreta become Lieutenant Harry Buford?

3. Which parts of Loreta's story do you think are true and which parts might not be true?

4. What is your opinion of women fighting as soldiers?

READING ON YOUR OWN

Behind Rebel Lines: The Incredible Story of Emma Edmonds, Civil War Spy
by Seymour Reit

Seymour Reit tells the story of Canadian-born Emma Edmonds, who disguised herself as a man and went behind Confederate lines to spy for the Union army.

Keeping Secrets
by Joan Lowery Nixon

Joan Lowery Nixon's novel deals with the activities of a young woman working as a Union spy in Missouri during the Civil War.

The Secrets of Sarah Wheelock
by Ann Rinaldi

Ann Rinaldi's historical novel presents the experiences of a Michigan farm girl who disguises herself as a boy to fight for the Union.

Charge on Cemetery Ridge

BY MARIANNE McCOMB

The two Confederate soldiers lay shivering in their tent. The day had been warm enough, but the slow drizzle outside the tent made the two men feel cold.

"I cain't get the picture of the battlefield out of my head," one of the men muttered. "All I see is the blood, the smoke, the men falling down where they had stood proud just a moment before—"

"Enough of that!" the other man said harshly. "Shut yer trap, Daniel, or I'll shut it myself."

The man named Daniel was silent for a moment and then continued to speak as if he hadn't heard. "I was in the middle of the lines— right smack dab in the middle. If I'd ha' been in the front, or in the back, or on the sides, I'd be dead like the rest of 'em."

At the climax of their attack on Cemetery Ridge, Confederate troops reach the Union lines.

Daniel was quiet for a moment. Outside the tent, he could hear the wounded soldiers screaming and moaning. Their cries made him shiver even more. No matter how hard he tried, he couldn't stop thinking about the day that had just passed.

They would beat the Union soldiers once and for all.

"When I first got here, to Gettysburg," Daniel continued, "I said to myself, 'God A'mighty this here is beautiful country!' There were rolling hills and wheat fields as far as the eye could see. But then—after the shooting started—it wasn't a bit pretty anymore."

Daniel had arrived in the tiny town of Gettysburg, Pennsylvania, on July 2, 1863. He came along with 6,000 fresh Confederate recruits from Virginia and their brave commander, General **George Edward Pickett**. Pickett had promised his men that they'd see some action soon. Their Confederate forces had already fought two battles at Gettysburg, he said. On day three of the conflict, they would beat the Union soldiers once and for all.

People and Terms to Know

George Edward Pickett—(1825–1875) Virginia-born general of the Confederate army. He is best known for the daring charge he led against Union forces at Gettysburg on July 3, 1863, known as Pickett's Charge.

After Pickett and his men arrived at the Confederate camp, General **James Longstreet** brought orders from General Lee. Pickett should prepare for a strong charge against the Yankees. Tomorrow, he had said, on July 3rd, Pickett and his men should advance toward the center of the Union defense. It was located a half-mile away on a hill known as Cemetery Ridge. Another division and two brigades would support them. Fifteen thousand men in all would go at the Union troops. One forceful push at Cemetery Ridge, Longstreet said, would cause the Union's lines to break completely.

* * *

At 1:00 P.M. on July 3rd, 138 Confederate cannons opened fire on Cemetery Ridge. They hoped to weaken the Union forces so that Pickett and his men could move in and take control of the ridge. The Yankees returned fire immediately. For the next two hours, the battlefield was filled with thick black smoke.

People and Terms to Know

James Longstreet—(1821–1904) Confederate general who was second in command to General Lee.

Daniel and the rest of Pickett's troops stayed huddled behind the cannons. They were waiting to hear the command to begin charging. It seemed that they waited a long time.

Finally, at around 3:00 P.M., Pickett rode over to General Longstreet. In a few minutes, he returned and ordered his men to move out. Pickett now commanded 15,000 soldiers in three long lines. When Pickett gave the order, the men began marching up toward Cemetery Ridge. Because there was a mile of open ground to cover, they moved briskly, with the flags of 47 regiments flying in the breeze.

As he marched, Daniel could see the Union forces lining up on Cemetery Ridge. A shot rang out from the Union side, and then another, and another. Because they were marching in lines across an open meadow, the Confederates were easy targets. Almost immediately, Confederate soldiers began falling.

With each step he took, Daniel felt himself squeezed more toward the middle of the line. He watched in horror as the Union soldiers fired at the front of Pickett's line. When those men had fallen, they fired at the next row, and then the next and the next. At the same time, Yankee soldiers moved to the

Battle of Gettysburg, Third Day, July 3, 1863

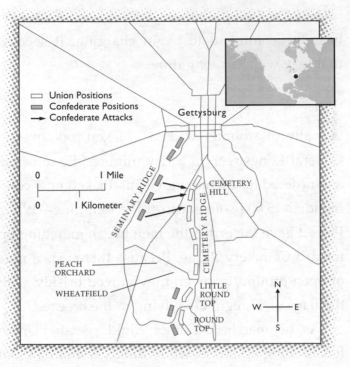

far corners of Cemetery Ridge and took aim at the last rows of the lines. Only a small group of soldiers in the middle were protected from enemy fire.

Soon the battlefield was littered with bodies. Daniel heard shouts, "Step over them! Step over them!" He and the others kept moving. Row after row of soldiers marched across the meadow while shells exploded all around them. Daniel had never seen anything like it. Nothing had prepared him for the terrible noise.

When he was just halfway across the meadow to Cemetery Ridge, Daniel heard the order to retreat. A commander on horseback galloped his way through the marching men and ordered them to turn around. "Fall back! Fall back!" he screamed.

Daniel stood still for a moment and wondered at this order. What had happened? Why weren't they going forward? All around him, men had turned about-face and were running back toward the Confederate camp.

"Are you an idiot? It's over! Retreat! Retreat!"

"Fall back!" another man shouted, this time right in Daniel's face. "Are you an idiot? It's over! Retreat! Retreat!"

Daniel turned around and found that he could not move a step. His eyes widened as he took in the scene all around him. The battlefield was covered with bodies. Everywhere he looked, there were rivers of blood. Some of the men who lay on the ground were crawling around in agony. Others were completely still. He watched as one wounded man got to his feet, staggered forward a few steps, and then fell to the ground again, his neck gushing blood.

▲
Dead soldiers after the battle of Gettysburg as photographed by
Timothy O'Sullivan, who worked with Mathew Brady.

Daniel began picking his way through the bodies. With tears streaming down his face, he followed the soldiers in front of him and kept his hands over his ears to block out the cries of the wounded.

When he arrived at the camp, Daniel dove into the first empty tent he could find. He lay on the hard ground, shivering and crying to himself. What on earth had happened?

Later, another man pulled himself into the tent and threw himself down next to Daniel. Daniel didn't know the man, but he began talking anyway.

"When I first got here, to Gettysburg," Daniel explained to the man, "I thought to myself: 'We'll see some action here. I'm finally going to have some fun and shoot a few Yankees.' But that ain't what happened at all. There was nothin' fun about this. The whole thing was ugly and bloody and awful."

"There was nothin' fun about this. The whole thing was ugly and bloody and awful."

"I'm telling you, boy, it ain't no good to talk about it," the man in the tent sobbed. "It's over now. Leave it alone."

"I cain't leave it alone, friend. I just cain't," Daniel replied. "When the fighting started, I realized that this war is about killing—nothin' more and nothin' less. I was in the middle of the lines, I tell you, but there was soldiers falling all around me. Those Yankees on Cemetery Ridge stood there with their cannons and muskets and waited for us to march toward them. It was like hogs to the slaughter, 'cept it was worse. There was the noise of the cannons and the screams of the men! No hogs I know ever died that way."

The man in the tent rolled onto his side and faced Daniel. The tears ran down his face. "I saw General Pickett himself," he said to Daniel. "Why, he was the bravest man I ever saw on a horse, but even he looked scared when the Yankees started shooting. He rode in front of the lines and yelled, 'Charge the enemy and remember old Virginia!'"

"I seen that, too!" Daniel said excitedly. "There was General Pickett with his tall hat and his fine horse, and behind him was a line of soldiers with their flags held high and their swords shining bright in the sunlight! I've never seen a sight that would equal that!

"But then, all of a sudden, everything changed. One minute everybody was ready for battle, and the next minute men were falling to their knees and gulping up blood. There were legless, armless, headless men everywhere I looked."

The two men lay silent once more. There was nothing left to say. The Battle of Gettysburg had been a terrible Confederate defeat. Their dead and wounded comrades lay in the rain in the middle of a blood-soaked field, their dreams were cruelly shattered. His mind numb and his heart heavy, Daniel finally closed his eyes to sleep.

* * *

General Pickett's charge was over almost before it started. Of the 15,000 men who assaulted Cemetery Ridge, 7,000 were killed, wounded, or captured. Almost all of Pickett's field officers were killed.

Overall, about 23,000 Union troops and more than 25,000 Confederate troops were killed or wounded at Gettysburg. General Lee blamed himself for the loss. This costly battle was the Confederate army's last major invasion of the North.

QUESTIONS TO CONSIDER

1. How does Daniel feel as he is preparing for the charge?
2. How does he feel after the battle is over?
3. What do you think went wrong with Pickett's Charge?
4. Why do you think that Pickett's Charge is famous?

The Long Road to Gettysburg
by Jim Murphy

Jim Murphy tells the story of the bloody, three-day Battle of Gettysburg, the turning point of the Civil War.

My Brother's Keeper: Virginia's Diary, Gettysburg, Pennsylvania, 1863
by Mary Pope Osborne

In Mary Pope Osborne's historical novel, 9-year-old Virginia witnesses the fighting at Gettysburg, the grim aftermath of the battle, and President Abraham Lincoln giving his immortal Gettysburg Address.

The Red Badge of Courage
by Stephen Crane

Stephen Crane's classic novel of the Civil War was first published in 1895. At that time, writers usually presented war as a glorious adventure. Instead, Crane tried to show what actually happens to soldiers in combat.

Glory for the 54th Massachusetts

BY CAROLE POPE

On May 31, 1897, the weather in Boston, Massachusetts, was overcast and misty. Sergeant William H. Carney of the 54th Massachusetts Regiment sat on the platform, listening closely. He held in his weathered hands the same flag he had carried at the Battle of Fort Wagner thirty-four years before. Carney was about to become the first African American to get the Medal of Honor.

Around Carney sat a small group of his fellow soldiers. Once young, many now had snow-white hair. Some walked with canes. Several were missing limbs. They were all there for the unveiling of the memorial honoring their heroic 54th Regiment, the best-known black regiment in the Union army. As

The 54th Massachusetts reaches the ramparts in the attack on Fort Wagner.

Carney listened to the words of **William James** and **Booker T. Washington**, memories of the Battle of Fort Wagner, South Carolina, came flooding back.

*   *   *

On January 1, 1863, President Abraham Lincoln had issued his **Emancipation Proclamation**. Now Northern blacks and freed slaves could join the Union army. In Massachusetts, Governor John Albion Andrew, a strong **abolitionist**, took quick action. He ordered a regiment of black soldiers, led by white officers, to be formed. It would be called the 54th Regiment of Massachusetts Volunteer Infantry. From all over the North, black men came to Massachusetts to volunteer. Among them were two

From all over the North, black men came to Massachusetts to volunteer.

People and Terms to Know

William James—(1842–1910) U.S. philosopher and psychologist. He gave the main address at the dedication of the memorial to the 54th Massachusetts Regiment.

Booker T. Washington—(1856–1915) influential black leader and educator. In 1881, he founded Tuskegee Institute, a school for African-American students.

Emancipation Proclamation—historic document delivered by President Lincoln on January 1, 1863. It authorized Union armies to free slaves in the South and led to the 13th Amendment, which officially ended slavery in the United States.

abolitionist—person who worked to put an end to, or abolish, slavery.

sons of the former slave **Frederick Douglass**, who now was a famous Northern speaker and abolitionist. Soon more than 1,000 men had swelled the ranks of the regiment.

On May 18th, friends, family, and officials were on hand as the men of the 54th Regiment prepared to leave for the island of Hilton Head, South Carolina. The men of the 54th were now a well-drilled unit. Carney smiled with pride as he remembered how they stood at attention in their brand-new uniforms, carrying **Enfield rifles**. They had been drilled to perfection. The 54th Regiment's white commanding officer, Colonel **Robert Gould Shaw**, accepted the colors from Governor Andrew. Knowing that these two men believed in the 54th, Carney and the other men were eager to prove themselves in battle.

People and Terms to Know

Frederick Douglass—(c. 1817–1895) famous Northern abolitionist, publisher, and speaker who was born a slave. Douglass advised Lincoln on matters regarding slavery and later became U.S. minister to Haiti.

Enfield rifles—bolt-operated rifles that were loaded behind the barrel.

Robert Gould Shaw—(1837–1863) Union officer. Son of Boston abolitionists, Shaw became commander of the 54th Massachusetts Regiment when he was 25 years old.

The 54th Regiment arrived at Hilton Head but received no further orders. Shaw and his men grew impatient. Hearing news of the war, they longed to join in the fighting. Things had been going well for the South. That previous December, Lee had won at **Fredericksburg**. In May 1863, he had won again, at **Chancellorsville**. Deciding to press his advantage, Lee decided to invade the North. He pushed into Pennsylvania, but, on July 3, Union forces at Gettysburg forced Lee's army to retreat to Virginia. The next day, General Grant forced a Southern surrender at **Vicksburg**. The men of the 54th saw that Union forces were beginning to win. Yet they sat on an island, waiting to go into action!

People and Terms to Know

Fredericksburg—Virginia town that was the site of a December 13, 1862, battle in which Lee's army defeated the forces of Union General Ambrose Burnside.

Chancellorsville—Virginia town that was the site of a May 1–4, 1863, battle in which Lee's army defeated the forces of Union General Joseph Hooker.

Vicksburg—Mississippi town that was one of the last Confederate holdouts preventing Union control of the Mississippi River. General Grant landed at Vicksburg on April 30 and cut off supplies to the town, which surrendered on July 4, 1863.

By July 6, Shaw had to speak out. He wrote to his commanding officer, General Strong, insisting that his men were capable of fighting bravely. Two days later, on July 8, Colonel Shaw got his orders to begin the march north to Charleston. The men were to take only blankets, battle supplies, and limited amounts of cold food, mainly hardtack. It was a long, difficult journey by foot and boat across the South Carolina coastal islands. Finally, standing between them and Charleston were four Confederate forts. The largest was Fort Wagner.

Finally, standing between them and Charleston were four Confederate forts.

Never had Carney seen a fort the likes of Fort Wagner. It was one of the largest earthen fortresses ever built. It stretched across the neck of Morris Island and was designed to protect Charleston Harbor. On its eastern side, high tide carried water up to the wall of the fort. The only approach to the fort was a narrow strip of sand, with a swampy marshland on one side and the ocean on the other. More than 1,300 Confederates manned Ft. Wagner. Log and dirt walls lined with cannons defended the fort from every direction. A three-foot-deep moat and rifle pit gave added protection.

54th Massachusetts, July 1863

SOUTH
CAROLINA

Charleston • Ft. Sumter
• Ft. Moultrie
Ft. Johnson • • Ft. Wagner

MORRIS
ISLAND

ATLANTIC
OCEAN

HILTON
HEAD

0   5   10   15 Miles

0   15 Kilometers

N
W—E
S

It was this heavily defended fort that the 54th Regiment was to attack. On the morning of July 18, Union battleships began shelling Fort Wagner. Their part was to "soften" the fortress for the land attack later that day. In the evening, 600 men of the 54th arrived at Strong's headquarters. Even though Strong knew they hadn't eaten real food for two days, he simply encouraged them and moved forward on the plan. Carney worried that Shaw and Strong might not understand how difficult it would be to take Fort Wagner.

The men of the 54th were given an hour's rest. Then they moved into position to lead the charge. Carney remembered Shaw's words to his regiment that night. "I want you to prove yourselves," he had said, with affection. "The eyes of thousands will look on what you do tonight."

"I want you to prove yourselves," he had said, with affection. "The eyes of thousands will look on what you do tonight."

The men were urged to ready their weapons, move quickly to within 100 yards of the fort, and then charge. With Shaw in the lead, next to the color-bearer who carried the flag, Carney and the other men tramped over the uneven sand. They searched the darkness for signs of the enemy. The only sound came from waves crashing against the beach and the gritty noise of their boots against the sand. To reach the Confederates, the men had to wade into the ocean, first up to their ankles and finally up to their knees. The path of the march grew increasingly narrow. The men were squeezed into a smaller line as they neared the fort.

At 200 yards, the enemy began firing. Carney would never forget the blinding flashes and the sound of men falling all around him in the darkness. Still,

Shaw urged his men to keep going. They did. Cannons boomed, and the men not yet hit moved toward the walls of the fort over their fallen fellow soldiers.

As the men reached the wall, they were picked off from above. Carney's last sight of Colonel Shaw was near the base of the fort. In the light of the gunfire, his face and sword turned upward, Shaw fell. Still, his troops fought on. In the face of almost certain death, they continued the attack. In the end, the dead were strewn for nearly a

In the end, the dead were strewn for nearly a mile.

mile. Soldier Lewis Douglass, son of Frederick Douglass, wrote his father about the bravery of the men in battle, saying "I had my sword-sheath blown away . . . swept down like chaff, still our men went on and on." The troops managed to enter the fort but finally they were overwhelmed and had to retreat.

When Carney saw that the color-bearer had been wounded, he grabbed the flag, holding it high. With wounds in both legs, his chest, and his right arm, he managed to return to the field hospital that night. When he staggered into the hospital, flag in hand, some of the wounded soldiers sat up and cheered. He told them that he had only done his duty: "The old flag never touched the ground."

More than 40 percent of the 54th Regiment were killed or wounded at Fort Wagner. The Confederates—angry at seeing a white officer leading black troops—stripped Shaw's body of his uniform. They tossed his body in a rifle pit and covered it with the bodies of his men. Later, Shaw's family was asked whether they wanted his body removed from the mass grave and shipped home for burial. Shaw's father said no. His son, he said, would have wanted no better than to be buried with his men, the soldiers he loved and respected so much, on the field where they fell.

* * *

Fort Wagner finally was taken by Union soldiers on September 6, 1863. In April 1864, the United States Congress passed an order making black soldiers' pay equal to white soldiers', mentioning in part the heroic deeds of the men of the 54th Regiment. In Lincoln's view, they had helped turn the war in favor of the Union.

Carney looked at the memorial, his journey into history complete.

QUESTIONS TO CONSIDER

1. What do you think motivated black men to join the Union army?

2. Why was Fort Wagner important to the Confederates? To the Union?

3. What did Colonel Shaw mean when he said the eyes of thousands would be upon them in their march on Fort Wagner?

4. How do you think the 54th Massachusetts Regiment should be remembered?

Martha Glover's Letter

The families of the black men who joined the
Union army often had a very hard time,
especially if they were slaves. Martha Glover,
a slave in Missouri, wrote this letter to her
Union soldier husband on December 30, 1863.

My Dear Husband,
I have received your last kind letter a few days
ago and was much pleased to hear from you once
more. It seems like a long time since you left me.
I have had nothing but trouble since you left. You
recollect what I told you how they would do after
you was gone. They abuse me because you went
& say they will not take care of our children & do
nothing but quarrel with me all the time and
beat me scandalously the day before yesterday—
. . . Oh I wish you had stayed with me & not
gone till I could go with you, for I do nothing but
grieve all the time about you. Write and tell me
when you are coming. . . .

Martha

Black, Blue, and Gray: African Americans in the Civil War
by Jim Haskins

Almost 200,000 African Americans, most of them newly freed slaves, served in the Union armies. Jim Haskins's account of these black soldiers shows how they helped win the war for the North.

Undying Glory: The Story of the Massachusetts 54th Regiment
by Clinton Cox

Clinton Cox presents the history of the first African-American regiment in the Union army.

With Every Drop of Blood
by James Lincoln Collier

James Lincoln Collier's historical novel tells the story of Johnny, a 14-year-old Confederate who is captured by a black Union soldier, Cush, a runaway slave.

A Confederate Submarine

BY DEE MASTERS

One of the most horrifying events in modern warfare is the sinking of a submarine. During the American Civil War, the Confederate navy lost one submarine—the *Hunley*—four times. The *Hunley* was very different from modern submarines. Instead of nuclear reactors, the *Hunley* was powered by the muscles of eight men turning cranks. It went about three miles an hour underwater. The *Hunley* was almost 40 feet long but only 3 feet 10 inches wide and 4 feet 3 inches tall. It was one of the first submarines ever built.

During a war, both sides usually try to develop new or superior weapons, knowing that these can help lead to victory. This was the goal

of the Confederates who helped to develop the submarine. Their story begins with a small, two-man submarine, the *Pioneer*. Early in the war, in 1861, a group of Louisiana planters, merchants, and inventors headed by Horace Hunley built the *Pioneer*. When the Union took New Orleans, the group had to destroy it. They barely escaped with their plans to Mobile, Alabama. Next, they experimented with an electric motor and a special steam engine. Finally, they settled on a design for powering the boat with a hand crank turned by four men.

The new submarine, the *American Diver*, was lost in a storm before it could be tested. Other Southern engineers and inventors quickly joined the project. The third submarine was finished in July 1863. They named it the *H.L. Hunley*. The *Hunley* was sent to Charleston, South Carolina, on two railroad cars.

The *Hunley* was made from a steam boiler. Tanks at the front and back could be flooded with water by opening valves. This would make the ship go deeper in the water. When they wanted the ship to rise to the surface, the crew could remove the water with hand pumps. The captain could use a lever to move two diving planes (wings) on the outside of the ship. Near the surface, two hollow pipes could be pushed up above the water to let in fresh air. The instruments were a mercury depth gauge, a compass, and a candle. If the candle went out, the oxygen was gone!

If the candle went out, the oxygen was gone!

When the *Hunley* arrived, Union **blockade** ships were firing on Charleston and not letting ships enter or leave. The South had just been defeated at Gettysburg and Vicksburg. Southerners feared that the tide of war was turning against them. General P.G.T. Beauregard, Charleston's Confederate commander, pushed the *Hunley* crew to attack. The crew felt they weren't ready. To Beauregard, this seemed like **insubordination**. He took over the ship and replaced the crew with inexperienced volunteers. Even worse, before the ship went into action, the officer in charge accidentally stepped on the lever for the diving planes. The submarine went down with the hatches still open. Five crew members were reported drowned.

People and Terms to Know

blockade—referring to the blocking of a place by military means, especially with ships, to control who goes in and out of it.

insubordination—crime of resistance to authority or refusal to obey.

On October 15, 1863, H.L. Hunley himself took the ship out on a training mission. She disappeared under the water as expected. She did not resurface. In heavy metal helmets and clumsy diving suits, divers finally reached the sunken ship. The front of the ship was stuck at a thirty-degree angle in heavy mud. The freezing water in the ballast tanks had spilled over the tops of the tanks. The shutoff valve handle had come off. General Beauregard described what he saw when the *Hunley* was raised: " . . . the spectacle was indescribably ghastly; the unfortunate men were contorted into all kinds of horrible attitudes; some clutching candles, evidently endeavoring [trying] to force open the man-holes; others lying in the bottom tightly grappled together, and the blackened faces of all presented the expression of their despair and agony."

General Beauregard did not want to use the "coffin" again.

General Beauregard did not want to use the "coffin" again. No Union soldiers had been killed. Fourteen Confederate soldiers had died in it. Lieutenant Dixon, the captain, argued that the ship was fine but the crews needed better training. Beauregard allowed Dixon to try again. The crew decided to see how long they could stay under water. The candles went out after twenty five minutes. The crew stayed down, though, for two hours and thirty-five minutes! They successfully came to the surface again.

B y February 1864, Charleston had been under Union blockade for two years. Months of repairs, changes, and successful undersea practice sessions had finally made the *Hunley* ready for battle. The submarine was designed to dive under a ship and pull a torpedo into the ship's side. But much of the water near Charleston was too shallow. So the plan changed. Instead, a ninety-pound charge of gunpowder would be fastened on the end of a long pole and driven into the enemy ship. The *Hunley* would pull back, and then the charge would be set off.

On February 17, 1864, at about 7 P.M., the *Hunley* moved slowly through the calm waters of Charleston harbor heading for a Union warship, the U.S.S. *Housatonic,* three miles from shore. The nine-member crew in their cramped vessel were sweating from the physical effort of moving the ship. They slipped through the cold winter night in the "coffin" that had killed two crews before them.

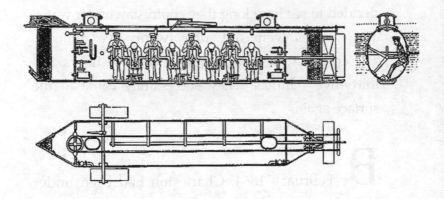

▲

This diagram shows how the *Hunley*'s crew propelled the submarine by turning a handcrank.

At about 8:45, an officer on the *Housatonic* thought he saw a dolphin swimming toward his ship. Other sailors noticed the strange object. The *Hunley* was too close for the *Housatonic*'s heavy guns to be turned on her. Sailors fired rifles and pistols, but the shells bounced off the submarine. The *Housatonic* pulled up her anchor and tried to back away. It was too late. There was a huge crash like a cannon firing. *Housatonic* crew members reported pieces of the ship shooting up higher than the mast. The *Housatonic* sank quickly in the shallow water. Most of her crew climbed to the masts, which remained above water. Five Union sailors were killed. The *Hunley* was the first submarine in the history of the world to sink an enemy ship during war.

Confederate soldiers kept a signal fire burning for the *Hunley*. After sinking the *Housatonic*, the submarine signaled with a blue light that the ship was safe and returning. But—

The *Hunley* and her crew of nine men never returned.

For 131 years the location and fate of the *Hunley* remained a mystery. In May 1995, the submarine was found four miles off Sullivan's Island in thirty feet of water. It had a "side wound" about five feet from the rear. On August 8 at 8:37 A.M., the sub was raised to the surface for the first time since 1864. It was taken to Charleston and put in a specially built freshwater tank. It is now being restored.

Confederate soldiers kept a signal fire burning for the Hunley.

The *Hunley* was far ahead of its time. Its feat—a submarine sinking an enemy warship—would not be repeated until fifty years later, when the British submarine *E-9* sank the German cruiser *Hela* in World War I.

QUESTIONS TO CONSIDER

1. Why was it important to the Confederacy to develop a submarine?

2. What problems did the inventors have to overcome in designing the *Hunley?*

3. What would have made the *Hunley* a bad assignment for a sailor?

4. Although the *Hunley* was the first successful wartime submarine, why might it be called a failure?

Burning a Path to the Sea

BY WALTER HAZEN

February 12, 1865
Barnwell, South Carolina

Dear Lily,

I don't know if this letter will reach you, but I had to write or go out of my mind. Dr. Culpepper agrees that writing is probably the best thing for me to do at the moment.

We have nothing left except the clothes on our backs. One week ago, the Yankees arrived in Barnwell. They've been moving north ever since they took Savannah on December 21st. Once they got to Barnwell, it didn't take them long to reach our place. When we saw them coming down the hill, they reminded us of a swarm

Sherman's troops destroy railroads and burn buildings during their March to the Sea.

of locusts. We had heard horrible stories about what they had done in Georgia. Were all these stories true?

The first thing I did before the **bluecoats** reached the house was to send Martha to her room. I told her to stay there no matter what. Thank goodness she is only six. Unless this first group of Yankees were complete monsters, I thought that she would be safe. I also sent one of the house servants to hide as much of our food as possible before they got here.

I'm grateful that, before he left, Hugh suggested we send Marsena and Fredericka to the nuns in **Columbia**. They are safe there, at least for the time being. But I worry about them all the same. A Yankee officer who also happened to be a gentleman told us that General **William Tecumseh Sherman** planned to burn Columbia to the ground. Time will tell if that will happen!

People and Terms to Know

bluecoats—term for Union soldiers, who wore blue uniforms.

Columbia—capital of South Carolina. During the Civil War, Columbia was a center of transportation and Confederate activity. Sherman's troops captured and almost entirely destroyed it in 1865.

William Tecumseh Sherman—(1820–1891) Union general who led 60,000 men on a March to the Sea that destroyed homes and property from Atlanta, Georgia, to Raleigh, North Carolina. Sherman's march began on November 16, 1864, and ended on April 26, 1865. Sherman's army's destruction broke the South's will to continue the war.

Lily, we had heard that Sherman's troops were burning and looting in Georgia. But we hoped they'd spare us, because none of our soldiers are in the area. Oh, we were wrong! They descended on us like vultures and took everything they could carry away. What they couldn't carry away or didn't want, they simply destroyed.

They descended on us like vultures and took everything they could carry away.

The first group of Yankees reached our house on February 6. They brushed past me and the servants and went straight to the kitchen. Everything that Jasmine had not hidden they ate within minutes. When they could find nothing else, they started destroying things with their bayonets. Pillows, mattresses, and featherbeds were ripped to shreds. Tables, dressers—even Hugh's guitars and the girls' violins—were jabbed and smashed. I'm glad Hugh was off fighting with his regiment. He surely would have tried to stop them, and he would have been killed.

While the Yankees were running freely through the house and taking what they wanted, I approached their commander. His name, I learned, was General David Hunter.

"General," I asked, "why are you treating us like this? We've done nothing to deserve such treatment."

General Sherman.

"I beg to differ," the general replied. "This is South Carolina. You are a South Carolinian. Your people started this terrible war. Now you're going to pay, and you're going to pay heavily!"

Wave after wave of Yankee troops marched by and pitched their tents on our lawn and in our fields. Soon there was nothing left for them to steal. Guess what they did then? They simply put the torch to the house! I couldn't believe my eyes! We all ran and hid in the woods until it was over. That was three days ago. Then those horrid soldiers marched back into Barnwell and burned the town to the ground. You can't imagine the scene! Only charred chimneys remain of the houses and buildings.

So, Lily, here we ·are. As I said before, we have nothing left. Thank goodness for the generosity of the Culpeppers. For some reason, the Yankees spared their plantation. We are staying there for the time being. I can't imagine what I'll do next.

She said it looked like the whole world was coming.

Did I tell you what I heard about Sherman in Georgia? Isabel wrote me several weeks ago from her plantation in Talbot County, Georgia, near Pleasant Hill. Her description of the approach of the Union troops made my spine tingle. She said it looked like the whole world was coming. First there were woodcutters clearing the way for the advancing soldiers. Then came men driving herds of cattle, followed by other men on horseback with turkeys and other things to eat. At the end came the troops.

Sherman's March, 1864–1865

NEW JERSEY

OHIO
MARYLAND
DELAWARE
ILLINOIS | INDIANA
Washington D. C.
WEST VIRGINIA
Richmond
Ohio River
VIRGINIA
KENTUCKY
MISSOURI
Raleigh (Apr. 14, 1865)
NORTH CAROLINA
ARKANSAS | TENNESSEE
SOUTH CAROLINA
Atlanta (Sept. 2, 1864)
Columbia (Feb. 19, 1865)
Mississippi River
ALABAMA
GEORGIA
Atlantic Ocean
MISSISSIPPI
Savannah (Dec. 21, 1864)
Sherman's March
LOUISIANA
FLORIDA
0   150 Miles
New Orleans
0   150 Kilometers
Gulf of Mexico

N
W   E
S

Isabel said the lines of soldiers stretched for miles. It took them the entire day to march by.

Some of them stopped at her place, though. They were brutish there, just as they have been here. They even dragged Isabel's mother all around the house by her hair! They tried to make her tell them where she had buried the jewels and silver. She refused, however, and after some time they left her alone.

Isabel said she had seen some "Sherman Pretzels." (Some people, I understand, call them

"Sherman Neckties.") What the Yanks do is tear up the railroad tracks, heat them over roaring fires to make them soft and flexible, and then wrap them around trees! I'm certain we shall see our share of Sherman Pretzels before this terrible ordeal is over.

I also heard from Nettie in Twiggs County, Georgia. Her letter was only slightly better. She said that when Sherman's men reached their plantation, she pleaded with them not to take all of their food. "Of a little, leave a little," she said to the captain in charge. He was a gentleman, she thought. What she meant was that, because they had so little to begin with, would they be so kind as to take only what they needed. The captain ordered his men to leave her family alone.

Burned buildings, houses, barns, and fences are everywhere.

I have heard of other such acts of kindness. To me, though, it seems that the Yankees are out to ruin us. I heard that Sherman has given his soldiers permission to destroy everything they see. You can't imagine what our lovely country looks like right now. Burned buildings, houses, barns, and fences are everywhere. Slaughtered cattle and livestock litter the roads and fields. Crops have been trampled under foot. The smell is unbearable. I hear that Sherman's path of destruction is 50 miles wide as he slowly winds his way through South Carolina.

Well, Lily, I shall close now. I'm so tired, and it's time to end my tale of woe. I hope you are lucky and are not in the way of Sherman's march. Everything points to the fact that he is determined to burn a path all the way to the sea.

Regards,
Maudie

QUESTIONS TO CONSIDER

1. Why did Maudie think that her family's plantation might be safe from Sherman's troops?

2. In what ways did Sherman's troops try to weaken the civilian population?

3. What explanation did General Hunter give for singling out South Carolina for special punishment?

4. What were "Sherman Pretzels"?

5. What is your opinion of Sherman's destructive March to the Sea?

Behind the Lines

Belle Boyd— Confederate Spy

BY JUDITH LLOYD YERO

Isabelle (Belle) Boyd was born in Martinsburg, Virginia (now West Virginia), on May 9, 1844. She was educated in Baltimore and went to her first ball in Washington, D.C. The outbreak of the Civil War sent her back to Virginia, where she became one of the most famous Confederate spies.

In her own words, Belle tells of her feelings and adventures.

* * *

"At sixteen my education was supposed to be completed, and I made my entrance into the world in Washington City with all the high hopes and thoughtless joy natural to my time of life. I did not

then dream how soon my youth was to be 'blasted with a curse'—the worst that can befall man or woman—the curse of civil war."

* * *

"The morning of the 4th of July 1861 dawned brightly. The Yankees were in complete control of Martinsburg. The village was at their mercy. We Martinsburg girls saw the Union flag streaming from the windows of the houses and felt just like the ladies of England would if they saw the flag of France floating above Windsor Castle. Those hateful strains of 'Yankee Doodle' filled every street.

"Those hateful strains of 'Yankee Doodle' filled every street."

"Whisky began to flow freely. The doors of our houses were dashed in. Our rooms were forcibly entered by soldiers who were 'mad drunk.' Glass and fragile property of all kinds was destroyed for no reason at all. They found our homes scenes of comfort, in some cases even of luxury. They left them mere wrecks. Shots were fired through the windows. Chairs and tables were hurled into the street.

"In some instances a trembling lady would beg them to spare some precious object—the portrait, probably, of a dead father. Words which no man with one spark of feeling would utter in the presence of even the most immoral woman were shouted in the ears of innocent, shrinking girls.

"A party of soldiers, known for violence, broke into our house. They had brought with them a large U.S. **Federal** flag, which they were now preparing to put upon our roof as a sign of their authority; but to this my mother would not agree. Stepping forward with a firm step, she said, very quietly, but strongly, 'Men, every member of my household will die before that flag shall be raised over us.'

"Upon this, one of the soldiers addressed my mother and myself in language as offensive as it is possible to imagine. I could stand it no longer. My anger was roused beyond control. My blood was literally boiling in my veins. I drew out my pistol and shot him. He was carried away mortally wounded, and soon after died. My little 'rebel' heart was on fire."

People and Terms to Know

Federal—relating to the U.S. government; here, Union.

Belle was arrested on a murder charge, but was found innocent. As time went on, Belle got to know many of the Union officers who occupied her town. She goes on with her story.

Belle overheard Union troops planning a trap for the Confederate soldiers.

"My acquaintance with so many of the Union officers helped me to gain much important information as to the position and designs of the enemy. Whatever I heard, I regularly and carefully committed to paper, and whenever I found an opportunity, I sent my secret information by a trusty messenger to some brave officer in command of the Confederate troops."

* * *

At another time, Confederate General Stonewall Jackson had advanced within a mile of Front Royal, Virginia, where Belle Boyd was staying. Belle overheard Union troops planning a trap for the Confederate soldiers.

"My heart beat alternately with hope and fear. I was in possession of much important information, which if I could only find a way to send it to General Jackson, I knew our victory would be secure. Without it I had every reason to expect defeat and disaster.

"I observed several men who had always said they were loyal to the cause of the South. I demanded if there was one among them who would dare to carry the information I possessed to General Jackson. They all with one voice said, 'No, no. You go.'

"I did not stop to think. My heart, though beating fast, was not fearful. I put on a white sun-bonnet, and started at a run down the street. These were crowded with Federal officers and men. I soon cleared the town and gained the open fields, which I crossed with great speed, hoping no one would notice me until I could make good my way to the Confederate line, which was still rapidly advancing.

"I had on a dark blue dress, with a little fancy white apron over it; and this contrast of colors, could be seen at a great distance. It made me far more easily seen than was just then agreeable. The fighting between the **outposts** was sharp.

People and Terms to Know

outposts—guards or small numbers of soldiers placed some distance from an army or camp to prevent surprise attacks.

"At this moment the Federal **pickets**, who were rapidly falling back, saw me still running as fast as I was able, and immediately fired upon me. My escape was most lucky. Although I was not hit, the rifle-balls flew thick and fast about me, and more than one struck the ground so near my feet as to throw the dust in my eyes. Nor was this all: the Federals, seeing the direction their pickets were shooting, followed the example and also opened fire upon me.

"Upon this occasion my life was spared by what seemed to me then little short of a miracle. Besides the numerous bullets that whistled by my ears, several actually pierced different parts of my clothing, but not one reached my body. Besides all this, I was exposed to a cross-fire from the Federal and Confederate **artillery**, whose shot and shell flew whistling and hissing over my head.

"At length a Federal shell struck the ground within twenty yards of my feet. The explosion, of course, sent the fragments flying, in every direction

People and Terms to Know

pickets—soldiers stationed to guard against surprise attack.
artillery—large guns or rocket launchers operated by a crew.

around me. I had, however, just time to throw myself flat upon the ground before the deadly shell burst; and again Providence spared my life.

"Springing up when the danger was passed, I continued my run, still under a heavy fire. I shall never run again as I ran on that memorable day. Hope, fear, the love of life, and the determination to serve my country to the last, all met to fill my heart with more than feminine courage, and to lend strength and swiftness to my limbs. I often marvel and even shudder when I reflect how I cleared the fields and bounded over the fences like a deer.

"I shall never run again as I ran on that memorable day."

"As I neared our line I waved my bonnet to our soldiers, to signal that they should press forward. On seeing this, one regiment gave me a loud cheer, and, without waiting for further orders, dashed upon the town at a rapid pace. They did not then know who I was, and they were naturally surprised to see a woman on the battlefield, and on a spot, too, where the fire was so hot. Their shouts of triumph rang in my ears for many a day afterwards, and I still hear them not unfrequently in my dreams."

*   *   *

Eighteen-year-old Belle got her message through. The Confederates won the day. General Jackson himself sent her this note. "I thank you, for myself and for the army, for the immense service that you have rendered your country today."

QUESTIONS TO CONSIDER

1. Why do you think it might it have been easy for Belle to get information about the Union army's plans?

2. What did Belle mean when she compared the way Martinsburg girls felt about the Federal flag to the way British women would feel about the flag of France flying above Windsor Castle?

3. Why do you think that the men "who had always professed attachment to the cause of the South" told Belle to take the message to General Jackson herself?

4. What do you think that you would have done if you had been a teenager in the South during the Civil War?

Spies in the Civil War
by Albert A. Nofi

Both the Union and the Confederacy used spies during the Civil War. Albert A. Nofi tells the stories of these men and women.

Sally Bradford: The Story of a Rebel Girl
by Dorothy Hoobler

Dorothy Hoobler's historical novel deals with the experiences of a young girl who must go far from her home in Virginia when her family's farm is destroyed during the Civil War.

Three Against the Tide
by D. Ann Love

Twelve-year-old Susanna Simons's father leaves the family's South Carolina plantation to serve as a Confederate spy. When Union troops invade the island, Susanna and her two younger brothers are forced to make a dangerous journey to find him. D. Ann Love's historical novel describes the children's adventures.

Songs to Lift
the Spirits

BY STEPHEN CURRIE

"Radios, stereos, compact discs," said the old man. "You young people today think music is so important, but you have no idea. If you'd been around during the Civil War, when my great-grandfather was a boy, you'd know how necessary music can be. General Robert E. Lee said, 'I don't believe we can have an army without music.' Well, he was right! During the Civil War, songs helped all kinds of people to survive—the soldiers, the women at home, and the slaves in the fields. I can tell you all about it, just as grandpa Hewitt told me."

*   *   *

Private Hill Hewitt wiped the sweat from his brow. It seemed like every day was a scorcher down here in Mississippi. His thick uniform didn't help

Although "God Save the South" was never officially adopted as the Confederate national anthem, it was considered so by many Southerners. (See page 10.)

matters any, either. He wondered how many pounds he'd sweated off during today's march. Five? Ten?

"What I'd give for a half an hour of rest," he murmured to the soldier next to him.

"Half an hour?" The other man gave a barking laugh. "What I'd give for five minutes. Five minutes and a sip of water, then I'd die happy."

What was the point of continuing the march?

Water—Hill tried not to think of the cool, sweet streams back home in Michigan. Instead he gazed ahead. The road—really nothing more than a trail through the thick Southern woods—seemed to stretch on endlessly. "How much farther?" he asked.

His neighbor shrugged. "I heard something about making it to the town by nightfall. That'd be seven, eight miles off."

Hill's body sagged. He'd never make it that far. Not in this heat. Not lugging around the enormous pack on his back. His pace slowed. His breathing became heavier. What was the point of continuing the march? Maybe he should just stop by the side of the road, even if it meant disobeying orders. Whatever happened to him couldn't be worse than seven or eight more miles of this torture.

"Hear that?" The man next to him jerked his thumb toward the front of the column. "The boys are singing. Let's join in, hey?"

Hill blinked and then listened. Sure enough, a melody came drifting back toward him. It was a familiar song. "Mine eyes have seen the glory—" The words had been written by a Northern woman named **Julia Ward Howe**. The song helped to remind the troops why they were fighting. The South had "Dixie" and "The Bonnie Blue Flag." The North had "Battle Cry of Freedom" and—

"Glory, glory, hallelujah!" came the determined sound from ahead.

"Glory, glory, hallelujah!" Hill chimed in, ignoring his weariness and his thirst. Other men nearby took up the song.

Hill marched on, singing from his heart. He stood straight now, the vicious heat and his heavy backpack forgotten. "His truth is marching on!" he sang.

Seven or eight more miles didn't seem impossible anymore.

People and Terms to Know

Julia Ward Howe—(1819–1910) Northern editor and leader in the women's suffrage movement. She wrote the lyrics for the song "Battle Hymn of the Republic" in 1861. (See page 10.)

*   *   *

"Of course," the old man continued, leaning forward in his chair, "it wasn't just the fighting men who sang the songs. No, indeed. The people at home needed them as much as anyone. Listen!"

Sadly, Sallie Jackson sat down on the piano stool. Another day and still no letter from Bob. Bob, her sweetheart, had gone off to the war six months earlier and was now fighting Union soldiers somewhere in Georgia.

Or so Sallie hoped.

When had the last letter arrived? A month and five days ago, Sallie thought, counting back. It had been a fine letter. Things were busy at the front, Bob had written, but he had not described the battles in any detail. Still, he had told her not to worry.

A tear formed in Sallie's eye. Why, of course she worried! How could she not be worried? To distract herself, she tried to remember what Bob had written about the soldiers' songs. Something about singing late at night around the campfires. Yes—that was it. "The songs make me think of you," Bob had told her. "We sing 'Lorena' and 'Tenting Tonight' and many more. For the women's names, I always substitute yours."

Slowly, Sallie's fingers moved to the piano keys. Striking a B-flat chord, she softly began to sing about a man going off to the war and a sorrowing woman left behind:

"Weeping, sad and lonely!
Hopes and fears so vain—
When this cruel war is over,
Praying that we meet again."

The last note died away, but Sallie felt closer to Bob than ever before.

* * *

"The slaves had their own songs, too," continued the old man, "and their own reasons for singing them. Songs might have been even more necessary for them than for anyone else. Here's why."

Dexter stooped low and faced the cotton plants. To the **overseer** halfway across the field, he knew, it would seem that he was working hard at picking the master's cotton. But Dexter wasn't picking. Instead, he was listening.

People and Terms to Know

overseer—one who keeps watch over and directs the work of others, especially laborers.

The field was alive with song. Near him, an old man sang a song that Dexter recognized as "Michael, Row the Boat Ashore." Farther down the line of pickers, three young women sang a bouncier melody, "Raise a Rukus." And somewhere in the distance he could faintly hear the strains of a slow, sad song called "No More Auction Block for Me."

The field was alive with song.

These songs were all very good, Dexter thought. They made the day go faster, and they could help to calm the soul. But the song he was waiting for had a different purpose. Where was the man he was looking for? Impatiently his dark eyes scanned the horizon.

"Follow the drinking gourd—"

The sound came from behind Dexter. Startled, he spun around, nearly losing his balance. Standing in the next row was a man with a wooden leg. *Peg Leg Joe*, thought Dexter, and his heart gave a lurch.

But he said nothing. It would be too dangerous to be seen talking to this stranger. Instead he turned away as if to continue his work.

People and Terms to Know

Peg Leg Joe—legendary African-American slave hero who led other slaves to freedom in the North.

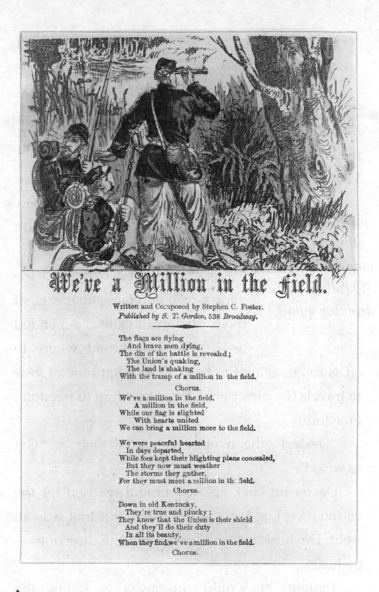

The patriotic Union song "We've a Million in the Field" was composed by famous songwriter Stephen Foster.

"For the old man is a-coming for to carry you to freedom," sang the peg-legged man softly, "if you follow the drinking gourd."

Dexter had heard of this Peg Leg Joe, though he had never before seen him. This man traveled Mississippi and Alabama giving slaves directions to freedom—in song, so that the masters never guessed. The drinking gourd was the **constellation** most called the Big Dipper. Dexter knew that a slave who followed it north might make it to freedom.

Tonight, he would run away to follow the drinking gourd.

Dexter listened closely to the verses, trying to remember each of them. His life, he knew, depended on it. The words told where to cross rivers, whom to trust, even what time of year to travel. The directions would lead him to freedom. Freedom!

"Dexter!" the overseer shouted angrily. "Get to work!"

Dexter bit back an answer and reached for the cotton. Peg Leg Joe had vanished, but that was all right. Dexter knew the song—and the directions— by heart.

Tonight, he would run away to follow the drinking gourd.

People and Terms to Know

constellation—group of stars that is seen as a recognized figure or design. The Big Dipper looks like a long-handled spoon, its lip points toward the North Star.

*   *   *

"Nothing like those old songs," the old man murmured. "Nothing like 'em today, that's for sure. Do you know what happened a few days after the war ended? Do you?" He didn't wait for an answer. "A Confederate officer told some Union generals, 'Gentlemen, if we had had your songs, we'd have whipped you out of your boots!'"

Smiling broadly, he leaned back in his chair.

"That's what happens, kids, when music is truly *necessary!*"

QUESTIONS TO CONSIDER

1. What emotions did songs like "The Battle Hymn of the Republic" spark in soldiers like Hill Hewitt?

2. How were songs like "Weeping, Sad and Lonely" helpful to those at home like Sallie Jackson?

3. Why do you think that slaves used songs to give directions for escaping?

4. How would you compare the importance of music during the Civil War to its importance today?

Some Songs of the Civil War

"Dixie"—rallying song for the Confederacy, though composed by a Northerner before the Civil War.

"The Bonnie Blue Flag"—patriotic Southern song of the Civil War.

"The Battle Cry of Freedom"—patriotic Northern song, sometimes called "Rally 'Round the Flag."

"Lorena"—sad song dating from before the Civil War but popular in both armies.

"Tenting Tonight"—melancholy song about soldier life during the Civil War.

"Weeping, Sad and Lonely"—popular song whose sheet music sold nearly a million copies during the war.

"Michael, Row Your Boat Ashore"—spiritual, or religious song, often sung by slaves.

"Raise a Rukus"—song whose verses express the slaves' desire to be free.

"No More Auction Block for Me"—slave song looking forward to a time of freedom.

Worse than Bullets

BY LYNNETTE BRENT

I joined the Union army on July 16, 1864. I was supposed to join a regiment going into battle. But instead, my first assignment was to guard Confederate **prisoners of war** at **Elmira Prison**. It seems that a train got into a terrible wreck bringing prisoners to Elmira. Sixteen guards and 64 prisoners were killed. They needed me to take the place of one of the dead guards. I was very disappointed. But they promised me that they'd soon find a replacement for me and send me to take my place on the battlefield.

People and Terms to Know

prisoners of war—soldiers who are captured by the enemy during war.

Elmira (el•MY•ruh) **Prison**—during the Civil War, Union prison located in New York, about 200 miles west of New York City.

Prisoners of war who died in camp are buried at the Confederate prison camp at Andersonville, Georgia, in August 1864.

Elmira Prison, New York

I couldn't believe what I saw at Elmira. To start with, most of the Rebel prisoners came without proper clothing or shoes. Because they were from the South, they didn't have heavy uniforms. Marching in worn-out shoes had given most of them sore and blistered feet.

Folks in town gave clothing for the prisoners, but the command at Elmira allowed only gray clothes. They ordered me to destroy clothes of any other color. Imagine how I felt! This left very few pieces to pass out to thousands of prisoners. Many wound up without shoes or decent clothing. Once cold weather came, they suffered greatly. Some prisoners had to stand ankle-deep in snow. Some collapsed from being out in the freezing temperatures. And when supplies finally arrived, only 2,000 blankets came for more than 8,000 prisoners.

At Elmira, prisoners died almost every day. It was a horrible thing to watch.

At Elmira, prisoners died almost every day. It was a horrible thing to watch. Many of these men were ill when they came to Elmira. Poor planning made matters worse. Prisoners were sent to Elmira too quickly. The government didn't have time to build enough rooms. The space for each prisoner was smaller than my clothes closet back home. Many prisoners lived outdoors, in tents. Because it was so crowded, diseases spread quickly. The Rebels—and many of the guards—caught smallpox, pneumonia, typhoid fever, and other diseases. When the war finally ended, I heard that nearly 3,000 prisoners at Elmira had died. I was lucky to have survived Elmira myself. Those poor Rebels didn't have a chance.

As awful as things were at Elmira, sightseers still came to watch the prisoners in the **stockade**. I couldn't believe what went on. Merchants sold popcorn and lemonade. An observation deck was built. Tourists paid money to climb the tower and look inside the prison walls. From there they could see prisoners crowded in the yard and the dead being taken away on stretchers. The whole thing made me sick.

You can't imagine how relieved I was when I received my transfer in February. Within a month, I was marching with my new regiment and General Grant toward **Richmond**. On April 3, 1865, we took

People and Terms to Know

stockade—jail on a military base. Originally, it was a defensive barrier made of strong posts or timbers driven into the ground upright and side by side. A stockade was often used to keep enemies out and prisoners in.

Richmond—capital of Virginia and capital of the Confederacy during most of the Civil War. In June–July 1862, McClellan failed to capture Richmond, but Grant took the city in 1865.

the city and captured many Confederate soldiers. We were told to take them to the Confederates' **Libby Prison**, which was located nearby. We freed the Union soldiers who were held there and locked up our new Confederate captives in the same cells.

I couldn't believe what happened next. My commander knew that I had been at Elmira, so he reassigned me—to Libby Prison, to be a guard again! It was my worst nightmare come true!

Libby Prison, Virginia

Libby Prison didn't seem too bad at first. Because of my experience at Elmira, Libby's commander gave me an important job—checking Libby's buildings to make sure that no prisoners could escape. I found that Libby's first floor held offices, a hospital, and a kitchen. Upstairs, prisoners were locked up in six rooms. Because there were no beds, they slept on the hard wooden floors. On cold nights, they had to sleep close together so that their body heat would keep them warm. I wondered how our commander was going to treat these poor Rebels.

People and Terms to Know

Libby Prison—Confederate prison that was located in Richmond, Virginia.

I went on checking the main building. To me, the first floor looked very secure. Its windows were small and protected by bars. At each door, two soldiers stood guard. And all doors inside the building were bolted so that no one could go in or out without a guard.

More than 100 Union soldiers escaped through this tunnel.

My main worry was the cellar. The commander had warned me about it. It wasn't used to house supplies or prisoners because it always flooded during a heavy rain. No one visited the cellar now, except the hundreds of rats that lived there. Whenever the cellar flooded, the rats could be seen swimming out the windows by the dozen.

This cellar was made famous by a group of Union soldiers who were held at Libby after the Battle of Bull Run. Colonel Thomas Rose and a few soldiers dug a tunnel from the "rat" cellar to an area outside the prison gates. The only tools they had were jackknives, an old chisel, a rope, and a wooden bowl. The bowl was used to move the loose dirt to a hiding place. By these means, they dug a tunnel that was over 50 feet long. More than 100 Union soldiers escaped through this tunnel, and over half of them made it to freedom.

Confederate prisoners at Libby knew the story of the tunnel. That's why my commander ordered me to find the tunnel and make sure that none of our prisoners could use it to escape. I spoke with a few Confederate guards that were now held prisoner. They told me enough about Colonel Rose's escape that I was able to retrace his steps.

In the Tunnel

I didn't like this assignment, but I had no choice. To enter the cellar, the Union soldiers had used a fireplace in the kitchen. They had chiseled out bricks to make an opening and then set them back loosely in place. I retraced their steps. First I tied a rope to a large beam in the kitchen. Then I climbed into the hole in the fireplace and, holding onto the rope, lowered myself into the cellar. The passage that had been cut by Colonel Rose and his soldiers was barely large enough to pass through.

I lost my grip on the rope and fell down the hole, landing flat on my back on the cellar floor. I could feel rats moving underneath me. More ran across my chest and legs before I could get to my feet. It took everything I had not to scream. As I stood up, I looked around the cellar. The floor was covered with straw and seemed to be moving

These three Confederates were taken prisoner at the Battle of Gettysburg.

because of all of the rats running around. It was terrifying, but I tried to ignore it. I would see plenty of rats today, I told myself.

I looked around the cellar. There was very little light, just a bit coming from the small cellar windows. I saw tunnel holes in a few places around the cellar. Colonel Rose had tried digging in a number of spots before finally succeeding. The Confederate guards said that Rose and his companions had dug only at night, working by candlelight.

I walked over to the corner of the cellar where the final tunnel was dug. The hole was small, like the one leading down from the kitchen fireplace. I wasn't sure what to do. Finally, I decided that I couldn't secure the hole unless I followed the tunnel myself. I took a deep breath, and then crawled inside the hole.

The cellar air was sour and sickly, but the tunnel air was much worse. Not only did it smell terrible, but it was very stuffy. When I crawled into the hole, my body blocked out the light. It became pitch black. I had to feel my way along. Soon I could hardly breathe. The space was so small that the oxygen was running out. I thought of Colonel Rose. I would only be in the tunnel for a few minutes. Colonel Rose had worked in the tunnel for hours at a time. I had heard that he had often become faint from lack of air.

I scrambled forward as fast as I could. Finally, I reached the end of the tunnel. What a relief! I found a board covering the exit hole. Was it secure, I wondered? I pushed against the board as hard as I could, feeling dizzy from lack of fresh air. The board didn't budge. Well, I didn't care anymore. I was going back to the kitchen. I couldn't turn around, so I began to back up instead.

But I was stuck. Something on my pants had caught on the side of the tunnel wall. I couldn't move my arms past my waist. I wiggled and twisted, but that only made things worse. The only way out was the boarded-up exit. I knew I wouldn't be able to lift the board myself. Instead, I began pounding with my fists. I prayed that someone passing by would hear me.

> *I crouched quietly in the dark, hoping that I wouldn't die there.*

It felt like I was pounding and crying out for hours. I had to concentrate on staying conscious. I desperately needed fresh air. I grew too weak to keep calling for help. I crouched quietly in the dark, hoping that I wouldn't die there. Finally I heard people talking. I thought I heard someone call my name. I tried banging on the board again, but there was no response. It must have been my imagination.

Then I felt something at my feet. At first, I thought it was the rats! I kicked and twitched trying to drive them away. But instead of hearing a squeal, I heard someone holler. I wasn't alone in the tunnel anymore. Someone was behind me tugging at my legs. I stopped fighting and held still. Finally I felt my legs give. I shimmied backward, trying not to bump into my rescuer. I was finally out of the tunnel.

We climbed up the rope ladder into the kitchen. My commanding officer was waiting there for me, along with four men that had formed a rescue party. I have never been so happy to see sunlight and breathe clean air!

After I recovered, I told the commander that the tunnel was secure. I was granted two days off. I was so glad to be freed from the tunnel that I slept outside under the stars both nights.

QUESTIONS TO CONSIDER

1. Why do you think that this story is called "Worse than Bullets"?

2. How would you describe conditions at Elmira and Libby prisons? What contributed to the prisons being the way they were?

3. Why do you think that visitors wanted to watch the prisoners at Elmira Prison?

4. How do you think that the prison system should treat prisoners of war? Should they be treated differently from other prisoners?

Clara Barton at the Battle of Antietam

BY BARBARA LITTMAN

It was one o'clock in the morning. Union and Confederate campfires could be seen flickering on the hillsides. A small figure crept past the Union artillery wagons. Women usually weren't allowed in the camps or on the battlefield. But the small dark figure was definitely a woman. In an unfashionable dark skirt and plain blouse, she made her way quietly to a man lying on the ground asleep.

She leaned down and shook his shoulder. With a start, he shot upright, his dirty blanket hanging off his shoulder. Then, with a sigh, he relaxed. It was Clara.

A Union surgeon performs an operation in a hospital tent at Gettysburg,
July 1863.

Cornelius Welles had never known anyone like **Clara Barton**. He had led her medical and provision wagons to many battles. He had seen this shy former schoolteacher give bread to the wounded along the way and use her own money to buy more for soldiers in the front lines of battle. He had seen her wring blood from her skirt after wading into a sea of injured soldiers to see who could be saved. He had watched her mix **gruel** to feed soldiers when she was so tired she could barely stand. Barton had saved many Union soldiers from starvation and freezing.

Barton also had started a movement to get citizens to donate food, clothes, and medical supplies. Donations poured in and the army **quartermaster** finally had to give her a warehouse to store them. This year, the warehouse had held about five tons of supplies most of the time.

People and Terms to Know

Clara Barton—(1821–1912) advocate for the needs of Union soldiers. After the war, Barton founded and led the American Red Cross (1881), helped with disaster relief, and helped the wounded during the Spanish-American War (1898).

gruel—thin, almost liquid food made by boiling oatmeal or another grain in water or milk.

quartermaster—army officer who is in charge of providing housing, clothing, fuel and transportation for troops.

That was what Clara was talking about now—the supplies. She asked Welles to help her move her supply wagons before the rest of the wagons started moving out. Usually, Barton's wagons traveled toward the back of the caravan. By the time they reached the battlefield, men had died and soldiers were hungry.

Welles agreed. By dawn, they were right behind the artillery wagons. Barton and Welles followed the wagons for a day, staying the night where the troops of General Ambrose Burnside were camped, across **Antietam Creek** from Confederate troops.

The next day was September 17, 1862. The fighting started early, just as the sun rose over the peaks of the Blue Ridge Mountains. The air was already thick with the smell of **sulfur** from the previous day's fighting. Barton didn't know it, but

---

People and Terms to Know

Antietam (an•TEE•tuhm) **Creek**—Maryland site of an important Civil War battle on September 17, 1862, that stopped a Confederate advance to Washington, D.C.

sulfur—light yellow, nonmetallic element that burns easily and produces a heavy odor. Sulfur is used in making matches, gunpowder, and other products.

the Battle of Antietam would be the bloodiest single day of the Civil War. More than 23,000 men would be killed or wounded.

This time, Barton's wagon was right on the battle-front, not three days behind. Hoping to help the most badly hurt, Barton and Welles followed the cannon in their wagon. Taking cover in a large cornfield, Barton found a clearing nearby where more than 300 wounded soldiers lay uncared for near a large, abandoned barn.

Clara Barton. ▶

Barton gathered bandages and medicine from her wagon. She was less than an eighth of a mile from the front lines, and artillery shells were bursting over her head. Muskets and cannons fired all around her. Smoke filled the air, making it hard to breathe and to see. As she carried her supplies toward the clearing, she saw a narrow trail leading out of the field. It looked as if men had recently walked there—or perhaps bodies had been dragged along the trail.

Barton followed the trail a short way. There, on the porch of an old farmhouse, was her friend, Dr. Dunn, operating on a soldier. The doctors had set up four tables as an operating room. Quickly, Barton set her supplies down nearby.

Dr. Dunn was excited to see Barton. Her supplies were badly needed. **Chloroform** was running low, and Dunn and the other surgeons had been using cornhusks for bandages because they had run out of cloth.

People and Terms to Know

Chloroform (KLOR•uh•FORM)—colorless liquid with a sharp, sweetish smell and taste. Its vapor can make a person unconscious or unable to feel pain.

All day long, Barton sent her men back to the provision wagons to bring supplies to the farmhouse and barn. She assisted with surgery and helped move men into the barn and farmhouse. Barton made sure that these places had fresh air and were kept as clean as possible.

At one point, Barton was almost killed! As she lifted her arm to give a wounded soldier a drink, a stray bullet went through the sleeve of her blouse. She didn't have time to give it much thought. The men had run out of food, and she had to make gruel right away.

As darkness fell, Barton saw that the surgeons had only a few short candles to light their work. She led Dr. Dunn to the barn. There, the interior was lit with lanterns from her wagons. The doctors were able to care for the wounded through the night.

For three days, the medical team worked almost non-stop. Finally, army troops arrived with new supplies. By this time, Barton was exhausted and sick. She had caught typhoid fever and needed a long rest to recover. She crawled into the back of her wagon, wrapped herself in blankets, and was taken home.

After she left, Dr. Dunn wrote his wife a letter about the Battle of Antietam and how one woman had made it possible to save so many lives. He called Barton "the true heroine of the age, the angel of the battlefield."

*　*　*

As the war went on, Barton continued to go to the battlefront where she fed and nursed the wounded. She was appointed superintendent of nurses for the army. In 1865, President Lincoln asked her to set up a program to find missing soldiers. Her office helped more than 22,000 families find missing soldiers.

QUESTIONS TO CONSIDER

1. Why did Clara Barton want to move her wagons up to the front of the caravan?

2. If you had been in Barton's place, what would you have thought was the most important thing you could do for wounded soldiers?

3. Why do you think Clara Barton is important in the history of the Civil War?

Clara Barton

On September 1, 1862, the Battle of Chantilly was fought during a fierce thunderstorm. Barton was with the Union forces:

"I was aroused at 12 o'clock by the rumbling of more wagons of wounded men. I slept two hours, and oh, what strength I had gained! I may never know two other hours of equal worth. I sprang to my feet dripping wet, covered with ridges of dead grass and leaves, wrung the [rain] water from my hair and skirts, and went forth again to my work.

"When I stood again under the sky, the rain had ceased, the clouds were sullenly retiring, and the lightning, as if deserted by its boisterous companions, had withdrawn to a distant corner and was playing quietly by itself. . . . Silent? I said so. And it was, save the ceaseless rumbling of the never-ending train of army wagons which brought alike the wounded, the dying, and the dead."

Getting By:
A Civil War Diary

BY MARIANNE McCOMB

From the Desk of Elizabeth Clayton

May 1863

Columbia

Honestly, if this war goes on much longer, I'll be ready to write that fool Lincoln a letter and give him a piece of my mind. Why, we are just barely getting by here in the South! It is time he knows what that feels like. The blockade here in Columbia is just a terrible nightmare that I can't awaken myself from. Added to that is the fact that nearly all the men on the plantation have now gone off to fight this horrible, horrible war. That leaves myself and the girls to manage the house, the servants, the fields, the bookkeeping, and everything else. It's almost more than I can bear.

And let me tell you, the slaves—they have been of absolutely no help at all. They keep carrying on about their **Day of Jubilee** and how they are free now. I know for a fact, though, that our slaves are not free. I know it because of what my beloved Colonel said, right before he kissed me good-bye. He said, "Now don't go freeing any slaves while I'm gone, honey." So I'm not about to pass out any freedom papers unless Colonel Clayton tells me to do so.

Jasper, the overseer of the field slaves, said to me today, "Miz Clayton, you've got to let us go now, or pay us wages." Can you imagine his nerve? I said right back to him, "Mr. Jasper, I'm not about to start paying wages or anything else. You people haven't even got the fields fully planted!" And here it is close to the end of planting season!

"Now don't go freeing any slaves while I'm gone, honey."

To tell the truth, though, the slaves aren't my biggest worry right now. It's the health and safety of the girls and myself that I worry about most. I promised the Colonel before he marched off that

People and Terms to Know

Day of Jubilee—many Southern slaves called the day Lincoln signed the Emancipation Proclamation (January 1, 1863) their Day of Jubilee.

I would take good care of the four of us. But I'll tell you, I'm finding that job more and more difficult with each passing week.

Today a neighbor came to call and told me of a terrible riot in Richmond, Virginia. It seems that the women and children banded together and stormed the stores. They demanded that the shopkeepers charge the women the same amount for food that they charge the army. When their demands were ignored, the women just took what they wanted. They said that it would be either "bread or blood"! I'm sure I feel the same desperation that these women feel. We are hungry, and there's just no decent food to be had.

The shopkeepers are taking advantage of us, I'm sure. Their prices are simply not to be believed. Because there is a shortage of supplies, they feel they have the right to charge anything they want. Yesterday at the butcher I saw a chicken advertised for $50.00! Can you imagine? This same scrawny bird would have fetched 50 cents before the war began. I do believe that some merchants are being just plain greedy. Ever since the start of the blockade, they've been holding back food and goods, and now the prices are outrageous. Although the

▲

After Savannah was captured by Union troops, Southern women received aid from the U.S. government.

Colonel did leave me a bit of extra spending money, I don't dare use it unless I must.

I must say, though, that I have learned to be quite resourceful. Because there is no medicine available, I have been experimenting with dogwood berries, blackberry roots, and other herbs. I use them to treat the girls and the slaves when they fall sick. Likewise, I burn corncobs to ash and use the ashes in place of baking soda to make the bread rise. I always swore that I could not live without coffee.

Now coffee is fetching $70.00 a pound. So, of course, I cannot buy a bean. However, my dearest friend Charlotte showed me her recipe for "homemade" coffee. She roasts a combination of browned okra seeds, toasted yams, and burnt corn. I manage to drink a cup of this brew each day.

My darling girls wear shoes made of old carpets and saddles from the stable.

As you might imagine, clothing and the like is very scarce in Columbia right now. This afternoon I am wearing a dress made of rough fabric, and I am lucky to have it. Many of my friends come calling in rags that are in the worst possible condition. My darling girls wear shoes made of old carpets and saddles from the stable. Needles and pins are not to be found. They have become as precious as gold.

General Lee has sent a plea to all Southern ladies to please send more bandages and supplies to the troops. So our sewing circle has been meeting twice a week now to sew bandages and gather **lint** to send to our men. In addition, I go each week to the central train station in Columbia to set up a refreshment area for the sick and wounded soldiers who are waiting for connecting trains. Lately, the women and I have been also providing these soldiers with a bath, a change of clothes, and a cot to rest on. It's the least we can do for these poor, broken men.

I hear that in the North, women have had to join the workforce and take jobs in the **munitions factories**. I saw a cartoon the other day showing Northern women making bullets for the Union army. The man who drew the cartoon thought the scene was funny, but I don't see a thing funny about it. I would go to work in a factory or anywhere else if it meant I could help my darling Colonel Clayton or my beloved South.

People and Terms to Know

munitions factories—places where military supplies such as guns and bullets are made.

QUESTIONS TO CONSIDER

1. What are some of the hardships that Southern families faced during the Civil War?

2. What is Elizabeth Clayton's attitude toward the slaves on her plantation? How is this typical of the Southern viewpoint toward slavery at the time?

3. What would you say is the tone of Clayton's diary entry? Support your answer with evidence from the story.

4. What is your opinion of Clayton's attitude toward the women who have gone to work in munitions factories?

If You Lived at the Time of the Civil War
by Kay Moore

Kay Moore uses a question-and-answer format to present American life during the Civil War era.

When This Cruel War Is Over: The Civil War Home Front
by Duane Damon

Duane Damon describes the effect of the Civil War away from the battlefields.

Amelia's War
by Ann Rinaldi

Ann Rinaldi's historical novel describes the home front during the Civil War. Young Amelia Grafton sees the ugly passions aroused by the war divide her Maryland hometown.

Freedom Coming

BASED ON INTERVIEWS WITH
FORMER SLAVES

A s the Union troops moved through the South in the months of war that came after the Emancipation Proclamation, they brought news of freedom to the slaves. Some 60 years later, in the 1920s and '30s, some of these slaves told their stories.

"I will never forget the day we were set free!

"That morning, we all went to the cotton field early. Then a [slave] on a horse rode out with a message from old Mistress at the big house. He says she wants Mr. Saunders, the overseer, to come into town. And Mr. Saunders left and went in. After a while, the old horn over at the overseer's house blew. We all stopped and listened, 'cause it was the wrong time of day for the horn.

"We went back to chopping. And there goes the horn again.

A group of former slaves works on a cotton plantation in 1879.

"The man in the lead row hollers, 'Hold up!' And we all stopped again. 'We better go on in,' he said. 'That's our horn.' He hollered at the head man, and the head man thought so too. But he said we'd ketch the devil from the overseer if we quit without him there. Then the lead row man says, 'Maybe he's back from town and blowing the horn himself.' So we lined up and went in.

"When we got to the quarters, we saw all the old ones and the children up in the overseer's yard, so we went on up there. The overseer was sitting on the end of the **gallery** with a paper in his hand. When we all got there, he said, 'Come and stand close to the gallery.' Then he called off every-body's name and saw that we were all there.

"Sitting on the gallery in a hide-bottom chair was a man we'd never seen before. He had on a big broad black hat like the Yankees wore, but it didn't have no yellow string like most of the Yankees had. And he was in store clothes that weren't homespun nor jeans. His hair was plumb gray, and so was his

---

People and Terms to Know

gallery—porch or walkway with a roof over it, used for sitting outdoors. This structure sometimes is called a *verandah*.

beard. And it came way down to here on his chest. But he didn't look like he was very old because his face was kind of fleshy and healthy looking.

"I'm thinking we'd all been sold off in a bunch. I noticed some kind of smiling, and I thought they were sure glad of it.

"The man says, 'Do you-all know what day this is?' He was talking kindly and smiling.

"We didn't know, of course. We just stood there and grinned. Pretty soon he asked again, and the head man said, 'No, we don't know.'

"'Well, this day is the fourth of June, and this is 1865, and I want you all to remember the date. You are always going to remember the day. Today you are free, just like I am, and Mr. Saunders, and your Mistress and all us white people,' the man said.

"'I came to tell you,' he said. 'And I want to be sure you all understand. You don't have to get up and go by the horn no more. You are your own boss now. You don't have to have any more passes to come and go.' (We never did have any passes, nohow. But we knew lots of other slaves on other plantations that had 'em.)

> *"Today you are free, just like I am."*

"'I want to bless you and hope you will always be happy and tell you you've got all the rights that any white people got,' the man said. And then he got on his horse and rode off.

"We all just watched him go on down the road. Then we went up to Mr. Saunders and asked him what he wanted us to do. He just grunted and said, 'Do like you damn please. But get off the place to do it. Unless any of you wants to stay and make the crop—you'll get half of what you make.'

"None of us knew where to go, so we all stayed. He split up the fields and showed us which part we had to work in. And we went on like we did before. We made the crop and got it in. But there wasn't any more horn after that day."

Katie Rowe, a former slave in Arkansas

"Soldiers, all of a sudden, were everywhere—comin' in bunches, crossin' and walkin' and ridin'. Everyone was a-singing. We were all walking on golden clouds. Halleluja!

> *Union forever,*
> *Hurrah, boys, hurrah!*
> *Although I may be poor,*
> *I'll never be a slave—*
> *Shouting the battle cry of freedom.*

"Everybody went wild. We all felt like horses, and nobody had made us that way but ourselves. We were free. Just like that, we were free.

"It didn't seem to make the whites mad, either. They went right on giving us food just the same. Nobody took our homes away. But right off, colored folks started on the move. They seemed to want to get closer to freedom, so they'd know what it was—like it was a place or a city. But me and my father stuck. We stuck close as a lean tick to a sick kitten.

"We knew freedom was on us. But we didn't know what was to come with it. We thought we were going to get rich like the white folks. We thought we'd be richer than the white folks

"We knew freedom was on us. But we didn't know what was to come with it."

because we were stronger and knew how to work. And the whites didn't and they didn't have us to work for them anymore. But it didn't turn out that way. We soon found out that freedom could make folks proud but it didn't make 'em rich.

"Did you ever stop to think that thinking don't do any good when you do it too late? Well, that was how it was with us. If every mother's son of a black had thrown away his hoe and had took up a gun to fight for his own freedom along with the Yankees,

Former slaves employed as wagon drivers during the Civil War.

the war would have been over before it began. But we didn't do it. We couldn't help sticking by our master. We could no more shoot him than we could fly. My father and me used to talk about it."

Felix Haywood, a former slave in Texas

"The news come on a Thursday. All the slaves were shouting and carrying on until everybody was all tired out. I remember the first Sunday of freedom. We were all sitting around resting and trying to think what freedom meant. Everybody was quiet and peaceful. All at once, old Sister Carrie, who was near 'bout a hundred, started in to talkin':

> There ain't no more selling today,
> There ain't no more hiring today,
> There ain't no pulling off shirts today,
> It's stomp down freedom today.
> Stomp it down!

"And when she said, 'Stomp it down,' all the slaves began to shout with her.

> Stomp down Freedom today—
> Stomp it down!
> Stomp down Freedom today.

"There was no more peace that Sunday! Everybody started in to sing and shout once more. The first thing you know, they had gone and made up music to Sister Carrie's stomp song. They sang and shouted that song all the rest of the day. Child, that was one glorious time!"

Charlotte Brown, a former slave in Virginia

QUESTIONS TO CONSIDER

1. What did Katie Rowe mean when she said, "I thought we'd all been sold off in a bunch"?

2. What did the Yankee mean when he told the slaves "You don't have to get up and go by the horn no more"?

3. What did Felix Haywood mean when he said he and his Dad "stuck as close as a lean tick to a sick kitten"? What does this expression tell you about the lives of slaves?

4. Why do you think that the slaves did not take up guns and fight for their freedom once the war began? What hints do you get from Felix Haywood's story?

5. How would you have responded if you had been with Charlotte Brown when Sister Carrie told her stomp song?

Freedom's Gifts: A Juneteenth Story
by Valerie Wesley

Juneteenth is an African-American holiday celebrated each year on June 19. It marks the day in 1865 when African Americans in Texas finally learned that they were no longer slaves. In Valerie Wesley's story, two young cousins in 1943 learn the true meaning of the holiday from their old Aunt Marshall, who was present at the original Juneteenth.

I Thought My Soul Would Rise and Fly: The Diary of Patsy, a Freed Girl
by Joyce Hansen

Joyce Hansen's historical novel presents the experiences of a 12-year-old African-American girl facing a variety of challenges, including her puzzling new freedom, in the months following the Civil War.

Forever Free: From the Emancipation Proclamation to the Civil Rights Bill of 1875
by Darlene Clark Hine

The Emancipation Proclamation was only the first step for African Americans in a very long road to fully gaining their freedom. Darlene Clark Hine describes the first part of that road, the Reconstruction Era.

Sources

Robert E. Lee's Decision *by Barbara Littman*

The people in this story are all real. Information about Lee can be found in *Recollections and Letters of General Robert E. Lee* by Robert Edward Lee (New York: Doubleday, Page & Company, 1904).

Unconditional Surrender Grant *by Stephen Feinstein*

Jonathan is a fictitious character based on information about soldiers' feelings and activities found in primary source materials. The details about Grant's campaign in February 1862, including the battles at Fort Henry and Fort Donelson, are historically accurate. Copies of the handwritten notes with Grant demanding and Buckner agreeing to unconditional surrender can be found in *Personal Memoirs of U.S. Grant,* Vol. I (New York: Charles L. Webster & Co., 1885).

The Other President *by Walter Hazen*

Both the journal entry and the journal writer are fictional. Details about Jefferson Davis's life are drawn from primary and secondary sources. The *Atlantic Monthly* article of 1864 quoted in the text is one such primary source. A good place to get information about Davis is *Jefferson Davis: Unconquerable Heart* by Felicity Allen (Columbia, MO: University of Missouri Press, 2000).

Mr. Lincoln's Humor *by Judith Lloyd Yero*

The source for these stories is *Abe Lincoln Laughing: Humorous Anecdotes from Original Sources by and about Abraham Lincoln* edited by Paul M. Zall (Knoxville, TN: University of Tennessee Press, 1995).

Civil War Soldiers *by Stephen Currie*

The characters and their letters in this story are fictional. They are based on real letters written by soldiers during the Civil War as well as on historians' accounts. Good sources for this information include *The Civil War* by Bruce Catton (New York: American Heritage Press, 1971) and two books by Bell Wiley published by Louisiana State University Press in 1994, *The Life of Billy Yank: The Common Soldier of the Union* and *The Life of Johnny Reb: The Common Soldier of the Confederacy.* Will Greene's letters are published in *Letters from a Sharpshooter by William B. Greene 1861–1865* transcribed by William H. Hastings (University Press of Virginia, 1993).

Loreta Velazquez Becomes Lieutenant Harry Buford *by Walter Hazen*

Maria, the writer of the letter, and Inez, the person to whom the letter is addressed, are fictitious characters. Loreta Velazquez is a real person who wrote a book called *The Woman in Battle* (Richmond, VA: Dustin Gilman & Co., 1876; reprinted by Ayer, 1972). To learn more about Loreta Velazquez, see Richard Hall's *Patriots in Disguise: Women Warriors of the Civil War* (New York: Paragon House, 1993).

Charge on Cemetery Ridge *by Marianne McComb*

Pickett's Charge is a real event documented in many accounts of the Civil War. Daniel and the unnamed men in this story are fictional characters. You can read real personal narratives in *Blood: Stories of Life and Death from the Civil War* edited by Peter Kadzis (New York: Thunder's Mouth Press & Balliett & Fitzgerald, 2000). For an overview of the Battle of Gettysburg, see *Gettysburg: Journey in Time* by William A. Frassanito (New York: Charles Scribner's Sons, 1975) or *Gettysburg: The Confederate High Tide* by Champ Clark (Chicago: Time-Life Books, 1985).

Glory for the 54th Massachusetts *by Carole Pope*

William H. Carney is a real historical figure. The story of the 54th Massachusetts Regiment was celebrated in the award-winning film *Glory*, directed by Edward Zwick and released in 1989. It is based on the letters of Colonel Robert Gould Shaw and Peter Burchard's *One Gallant Rush: Robert Gould Shaw and His Brave Black Regiment* (New York: St. Martin's, 1965). Two other sources of information about Shaw and the 54th are *Where Death and Glory Meet: Robert Gould Shaw and the 54th Massachusetts Infantry* by Russell Duncan (Athens, GA: University of Georgia Press, 1999) and *Lay This Laurel* by Richard Benson (New York: Eakins Press, 1973).

A Confederate Submarine *by Dee Masters*

The story of the *Hunley* is factual. You can find out more about the *Hunley* at the U.S. Navy's Naval Historical Center home page. Other sources include *CSS Hunley: The Greatest Undersea Adventure of the Civil War* by Richard Bak and *The Hunley: Submarines, Sacrifice, and Success in the Civil War* by Mark R. Ragan (Charleston, SC: Narwhal Press, Inc., 1999).

Burning a Path to the Sea *by Walter Hazen*

Maudie, Lily, and Isabel are fictional characters. Their stories are based on stories and diary entries found in books such as Katharine M. Jones's *When Sherman Came: Southern Women and the Great March* (New York: Bobbs-Merrill, 1964). The details about Barnwell, South Carolina, and about Sherman's March to the Sea are historically accurate. In February 1865, Sherman's General David Hunter had a conversation at the home of a Barnwell plantation owner that was very like the one given in this story.

Belle Boyd—Confederate Spy *by Judith Lloyd Yero*

The words of Belle Boyd are adapted from her book, *Belle Boyd in Camp and Prison* by Belle Boyd (Baton Rouge, LA: Louisiana State University Press, 1997).

Songs to Lift the Spirits *by Stephen Currie*

The old man, Private Hill Hewitt, Sallie Jackson, and Dexter are fictional characters. Peg Leg Joe is legendary. Information about the songs of the Civil War is historically accurate. If you want to read more, author Stephen Currie has written a book called *Music in the Civil War* (Cincinnati: Betterway Books, 1992).

Worse than Bullets *by Lynnette Brent*

This story's narrator is a fictional character. The details regarding Elmira and Libby prisons are accurate, including the scary and suspenseful "digging incident." The details of this story can be found in *The Tragedy of Libby and Andersonville Prison Camps: A Study of Mismanagement and Inept Logistical Policies at Two Southern Prisoner-of-War Camps during the Civil War* by Daniel Patrick Brown (Ventura, CA: Golden West Historical Publications, 1988.)

Clara Barton at the Battle of Antietam
by Barbara Littman

Cornelius Welles, Dr. Dunn, and Clara Barton are all real historical figures. Barton's activities at the Battle of Antietam are well documented. Most libraries for students have many books about her. A good adult source is *Clara Barton: Professional Angel* by Elizabeth Brown Pryor (Philadelphia: University of Pennsylvania Press, 1987).

Getting By: A Civil War Diary *by Marianne McComb*

Elizabeth Clayton and her journal entry are fictional. Southern women did keep diaries, however. Three good ones are *Through Some Eventful Years* by Susan Bradford (Macon, GA: J. W. Burke Company, 1926); *A Civil War Diary* by Mary Boykin Chesnut (Random House reprint, 1997); and *A Diary with Reminiscences of the War and Refugee Life in the Shenandoah Valley, 1860–1865* by Hunter McDonald (Nashville, TN: Cullom & Gertner, 1934).

Freedom Coming *based on interviews with former slaves*

During the Great Depression of the 1930s, writers interviewed former slaves to produce a written record of their historic experiences. The three accounts given here are from those interviews. Only the spelling and grammar have been modernized. They can be found in *Remembering Slavery: African Americans Talk about Their Personal Experiences of Slavery and Emancipation* edited by Ira Berlin, Marc Favreau, and Steven F. Miller (New York: The New Press, in association with The Library of Congress, Washington, D.C., 1998).

Glossary of People and Terms to Know

abatis (AB•UH•tihs)—barricade formed by stacking cut-down trees with sharpened branches to stop the advance of the enemy.

abolitionist—person who worked to put an end to, or abolish, slavery.

Antietam (an•TEE•tuhm) **Creek**—Maryland site of an important battle that stopped a Confederate advance to Washington, D.C., in September 1862.

artillery—large guns or rocket launchers operated by a crew.

Barton, Clara—(1821–1912) advocate for the needs of Union soldiers during the Civil War. Barton founded and led the American Red Cross (1881), helped with disaster relief, and helped the wounded during the Spanish-American War (1898).

bayonet (BAY•uh•net)—stabbing weapon attached to a long gun. The bayonet was a long, tapering, steel blade.

Beauregard, P.G.T. (BO•rih•GAHRD)—(1818–1893) Confederate general who commanded the attack on Ft. Sumter that opened the Civil War. He also distinguished himself at the First Battle of Bull Run, at Shiloh, and in defending Charleston. Finally, he was driven out of Charleston by General Sherman.

Black Hawk War—(1832) series of battles with the Sac and Fox Indians of Illinois. U.S. policy was to remove the Indians east of the Mississippi to lands to the west. When the Indian leader Black Hawk brought his people back, war broke out.

blockade—blocking of a place by military means (especially with ships) to control what goes in and out. Union forces blockaded Southern shipping ports, causing terrible shortages.

bluecoats—term for Union soldiers, who wore blue uniforms.

brigadier (BRIG•uh•DEER)—general who commands a brigade, a military group of between 1,800 and 2,000 infantry soldiers.

Buckner, Simon Bolivar (boh•LEE•vahr)—(1823–1914) Confederate general and later, governor of Kentucky from 1887 to 1891.

Bull Run—see First Battle of Bull Run.

Burnside, Ambrose E.—(1824–1881) former firearms manufacturer who became a Union general. Burnside commanded troops at Bull Run and at Antietam. In November 1862, Lincoln named Burnside commanding general. Later he resigned after failing to win an important battle.

cabinet—group of officials who head the major departments of government and advise the president.

cannon—large gun, especially one that is too large to be carried by hand, that is fixed to the ground or mounted on wheels.

Chancellorsville—Virginia town that was the site of a May 1–4, 1863, battle in which Lee's army defeated the forces of Union General Joseph Hooker.

chloroform (KLOR•uh•FORM)—colorless liquid with a sharp, sweetish smell and taste. Its vapor can make a person unconscious or unable to feel pain.

Columbia—capital of South Carolina. During the war, Columbia was a center of transportation and Confederate activity. Sherman's troops captured and almost entirely destroyed it in 1865.

Confederate States of America—government formed by the eleven states that withdrew, or seceded, from the Union during the Civil War.

constellation—group of stars that is seen as a recognized figure or design. The Big Dipper looks like a long-handled spoon, its lip points toward the North Star.

Davis, Jefferson—(1808–1889) president of the Confederate States of America, serving from 1861 to 1865.

Day of Jubilee—many Southern slaves called the day Lincoln signed the Emancipation Proclamation (January 1, 1863) their Day of Jubilee.

Douglas, Stephen A.—(1813–1861) famous speaker who served both as representative and senator from Illinois. Lincoln debated Douglas when he ran for Douglas's Senate seat.

Douglass, Frederick—(c. 1817–1895) famous Northern abolitionist, publisher, and speaker who was born a slave. He advised Lincoln on slavery and later became U. S. minister to Haiti.

Early, Jubal—(1816–1894) Confederate general. Like General Lee he was against secession but was loyal to Virginia. He stayed a Rebel all his life and never promised loyalty to the United States after the war.

Elmira (el•MY•ruh) **Prison**—Union prison located in New York, about 200 miles west of New York City.

Emancipation Proclamation—historic document delivered by President Lincoln on January 1, 1863, that authorized Union armies to free slaves in the South. It led to the 13th Amendment, which officially ended slavery in the United States.

Enfield rifles—bolt-operated rifles that were loaded behind the barrel.

Federal—relating to the U.S. government; at the time covered in this book, to the Union.

First Battle of Bull Run—Civil War battle fought on July 21, 1861, at Bull Run Creek in Virginia, 25 miles southwest of Washington, D.C. Here Confederate General P.G.T. Beauregard defeated Union soldiers under General Irvin McDowell, but did not go after them as they retreated to Washington.

Fort Sumter—fort at the mouth of the harbor of Charleston, South Carolina. Here the first shots of the Civil War were fired on April 12, 1861.

Fredericksburg—Virginia town that was the site of a December 13, 1862, battle in which Lee's army defeated the forces of Union General Ambrose Burnside.

gallery—porch or walkway with a roof over it, used for sitting outdoors. This structure is also called a *verandah*.

gangrene (GANG•green)—death and decay of body tissue due to loss of blood supply.

Gettysburg—Pennsylvania site of a major battle of the Civil War, fought July 1–3, 1863. Union forces under General George G. Meade defeated Lee, forcing him to retreat. The Union side lost about 23,000 men, the Confederate side about 25,000. This Union victory was a turning point in the war.

Grant, Ulysses S.—(1822–1885) commander of the Union army. 18th president of the U.S. from 1869 to 1877. Grant led Union forces to victory, but his presidency was marked by many scandals.

gruel—thin, almost liquid food made by boiling oatmeal or another grain in water or milk.

hardtack—dry bread made of flour and water. Soldiers on both sides of the conflict often ate hardtack.

Howe, Julia Ward—(1819–1910) Northern editor and leader in the women's suffrage movement. She wrote the lyrics for the song "Battle Hymn of the Republic" in 1861.

insubordination—crime of resistance to authority or refusal to obey.

ironclads—naval ships of the mid-1800s. Ironclads were protected with iron plates on the sides. Famous Civil War ironclads were the *Monitor* and the *Merrimack*.

Jackson, Thomas "Stonewall"—(1824–1863) U.S. general widely considered one of the best Confederate commanders. He received the nickname "Stonewall" at the First Battle of Bull Run (1861). There, his troops stood against the Union forces "like a stone wall."

James, William—(1842–1910) U.S. philosopher and psychologist who gave the main address at the dedication of the memorial to the 54th Massachusetts Regiment.

Kentucky—border state between North and South. Kentucky stayed in the Union, but many people there felt loyal to the South.

Lee, Robert E.—(1807–1870) commander of the Southern armies during the Civil War and a Confederate hero.

Libby Prison—Confederate Civil War prison located in Richmond, Virginia.

Lincoln, Abraham—(1809–1865) 16th president of the United States (1861–1865). When Lincoln's election was announced, South Carolina seceded from the Union.

lint—tiny bits of thread or fluff from any material. During the Civil War, wet lint was used to cover soldiers' wounds.

Longstreet, James—(1821–1904) Confederate general who was second in command to General Lee.

McClellan, George B.—(1826–1885) U.S. general and commander of the Union army during the first year of the Civil War. Though McClellan did an exceptional job of organizing and training the army, Lincoln dismissed him for being too cautious.

Mexican War—(1846–1848) war between Mexico and the United States. The war began when Mexico refused to accept the United States' 1845 annexation of Texas. After winning the war, the United States acquired Mexican territory from the Rio Grande to the Pacific coast.

morale (muh•RAL)—mental outlook, spirit, or confidence. The morale of a group of people is important to its success. A leader helps to keep people's morale high.

munitions factories—places where military supplies such as guns and ammunition are made.

musket—long gun used from the 1500s to the 1800s. The musket's single lead ball was fired by lighting a powder charge. Muskets were more than 5 feet long, weighed up to 40 pounds, and were not accurate beyond 100 yards.

outpost—guard or small number of soldiers placed some distance from an army or camp to prevent surprise attacks.

overseer—one who keeps watch over and directs the work of others, especially laborers.

pass—document giving permission to leave Union territory and enter Confederate territory. Passes were required for travel during times of war.

Peg Leg Joe—legendary African-American slave hero who led other slaves to freedom in the North.

pickets—soldiers stationed to guard against surprise attack.

Pickett, George Edward—(1825–1875) Confederate army general best known for the daring charge he led against Union forces at Gettysburg on July 3, 1863, now known as Pickett's Charge.

prisoners of war—soldiers who are captured by the enemy during war.

Quaker—name given to a member of the Society of Friends, a religious group.

quartermaster—army officer who is in charge of providing housing, clothing, fuel, and transportation for troops.

rebels—those who fight against the legal government. In this book, *Rebels* means soldiers in the Confederate army, who fought to create a separate nation.

regiment—military unit or body of troops.

reveille (REV•uh•le)—bugle call used to awaken soldiers.

Richmond—capital of Virginia and capital of the Confederacy during most of the Civil War. Grant captured the city in 1865.

Scott, Winfield—(1786–1866) U.S. army officer who was a hero of the War of 1812 and the Mexican War. When the Civil War broke out, the 75-year-old Scott briefly commanded the Union army but soon retired.

secede (sih•SEED)—withdraw from the Union. Some Southern states believed they had the right to separate from the United States and form their own national government.

secessionist— (sih•SEHSH•uh•nist) person who favored leaving the Union.

Shaw, Robert Gould— (1837–1863) Union officer, a son of Boston abolitionists, who became commander of the 54th Massachusetts Regiment when he was 25 years old.

Sherman, William Tecumseh— (1820–1891) Union general who with 60,000 men led a March to the Sea that destroyed homes and property from Atlanta, Georgia, to Durham, North Carolina. Sherman's march began on November 16, 1864, and ended on April 26, 1865. The destruction it brought broke the South's will to continue the war.

skirmishers—small groups of soldiers who stage attacks on enemy scouts or patrollers.

Stanton, Edwin M.—(1814–1869) U.S. Secretary of War under two presidents, Lincoln and Andrew Johnson.

Stephens, Alexander— (1812–1883) vice-president of the Confederate States of America. As a U.S. representative from Georgia, Stephens opposed secession but sided with the South when Georgia left the Union.

stockade—defensive barrier made of strong posts or timbers driven into the ground upright and side-by-side often used as a military jail.

sulfur—light yellow, nonmetallic element that burns easily and produces a heavy odor. It is used in making matches, gunpowder, and other substances.

Taylor, Zachary—(1784–1850) 12th president of the United States, serving only one year (1849–1850) before dying of a stomach ailment. Taylor had been an army hero, called "Old Rough and Ready" by his troops.

Union—states that remained in the United States of America during the Civil War.

Vicksburg—Mississippi town that was one of the last Confederate holdouts preventing Union control of the Mississippi River. General Grant landed at Vicksburg on April 30 and cut off supplies to the town, which surrendered on July 4, 1863.

Washington, Booker T.— (1856–1915) influential black leader and educator. In 1881, he founded Tuskegee Institute, a school for African-American students.

Yankee—word used during the Civil War to describe all Northerners and Union soldiers. In the Revolutionary War, the British called the American patriots *Yankees*. The Americans adopted the term. Today, *Yankees* means people from the New England states of Maine, New Hampshire, Vermont, Massachusetts, Rhode Island, and Connecticut.

Acknowledgements

10, 12, 18, 20, 22–23, 27, 33, 38, 42, 47, 50, 52, 62, 65, 69, 73, 80, 83, 85, 90, 92, 98, 102, 104, 115 Courtesy Library of Congress. 117, 122 (http://www.chinfo. navy.mil) — The U.S. Navy Office of Information.

126, 129, 137, 145, 147, 153, 158, 164 Courtesy Library of Congress. 169 © Corbis. 172, 178, 181, 185, 187, 192, 195 Courtesy Library of Congress.